DEAR FRIEND

Richard Allen

LOCK

&

KEY

RICHARD L. ALLEN

American Literary Press, Inc.
Five Star Special Edition
Baltimore, Maryland

Lock & Key

Library of Congress
Cataloging in Publication Data
ISBN 1-56167-830-9

Library of Congress Card Catalog Number:
2004090462

Published by

American Literary Press, Inc.
Five Star Special Edition
8019 Belair Road, Suite 10
Baltimore, Maryland 21236

Manufactured in the United States of America

Contents

THANKING GOD

I would like to take this opportunity to **THANK GOD FOR BEING WHO HE IS,** and there are no greater words I can say. I want to also **THANK HIM FOR HIS PRESENCE AND FOR ALL HE HAS DONE FOR ALL OF HUMANITY.**

I'm also asking **GOD FOR HIS FORGIVENESS** for some of the language in this book and to allow anyone I've offended to find it in their hearts to forgive me. Especially with the use of the "F—" word, I use friend, friendly or my friend in place of the street meaning of "F—" or "M—f—," throughout the book. I also understood "F—" to mean Fornication Under the Consent of the King. Back in the days when The Romans ran the show, weary soldiers after a long battle had to get permission from their earthly king to have unmarried sex. That form of battlefield relief was shortened to the four letter word as we know it today. But remember if someone asks you what word begins with "F" ends with a "K" and has "U C" in between the "F" and "K", you can respond with a correct answer—fire truck. No disrespect to Newark, New Jersey's bravest (fire fighters) equipment or any other of our proud country's fire fighters. Which reminds me of the crime fighter/cop that pulled over a speeding female motorist and asked her, "Where's the fire?"

She replied with, "I'm sitting on it."

Now while I have your smiling attention, did you all know that crime fighters and fire fighters both rely on some form of water in fighting crime and fires? Fire fighters obviously fight fires with water and crime fighters fight crime with just ice (better known as justice).

Whether it's street, courtroom, or jail house justice, crime fighters are always somewhere in the mix, mixing it up. Justice, at times, while living up to its name can be ice cold, which may be why our court room judges are so cool and calm under those long black robes. They often mete out justice in its purest, coldest, and fairest form. They are the master dispensers of justice and can at times seem hard and cold. At other times, not cold and hard enough, maybe due to some of that ice beginning to melt.

Not to intentionally slip away or down from discussing justice, does anyone know why court room judges wear black? Check this out: Black clothing knocks off ten pounds from your appearance right then and there, some Newark, N.J. court room judges can use that instant reduction in weight appearance and others can get your attention without pounding on the bar.

Since municipal court was my first home during my police career, I had the pleasing opportunity to personally notice a few of the female judges who were holding pretty well (with or without the robes) that went well with their professional demeanor. I'm pleading the fifth amendment concerning the male judges' appearances at this time. Thank you and continue to serve justice. May this book become enjoyment, knowledge, education, and hopefully, inspiration to all.

To all of the police officers throughout the world, it only takes less than a second to say **"GOD BE WITH ME"** prior to every assignment, so that you will safely come home after every assignment. There's no ill will toward any police officer mentioned or not mentioned in this book, everything that happened in this book or anyplace else in the world, happened for a reason.

The Enclosed Material

The enclosed material is true and actual accounts as they happened in the author's life primarily while serving the City of Newark, New Jersey, as a patrolman/police officer and in The United States Air Force Reserves as an aircraft mechanic and flight engineer. The title is in memory of a close friend and deceased South District Police Precinct/Station Police Officer.

He often called an ex-partner of mine and myself Lock and Key for our dog tired pursuit of criminals. Even though after he passed on, I eventually had to arrest his street corner merchant son/stepson, who was constantly involved in unlawful pharmaceutical activities on and/or near Bergen Street and Lyons Avenue. His criminal behind son also stole a police officer's hat/wreath from a store on Bergen St. While the one man officer on foot patrol was in the store briefly, removed his hat to cool off his hot head and turned his back to make an entry onto his foot officer's log sheet. Remember officers don't become "Hot headed," you made lose something, and if you have had any police equipment that mysteriously disappeared in the above area, the above police memorabilia collecting suspect is probably the drug dealing culprit.

Unlawful drug dealers and users are no better off than the Hitlers or any other of the mass murderers or killers, who were shamefully born, who filtered mass hurt and destruction throughout the world. Drug dealers and/or runners have no one to blame but themselves along with their cowardly greed and lust, which will be totally satisfied in hell. Drug users attempt to look around and lay blame elsewhere. I compare their elsewhere laying blame to starting a hot fire in a garbage can. We're all aware of what will happen if we place our hand in that garbage can of burning fire. It doesn't matter who started the fire or placed the garbage can there. All that matters is why would you reach in on your own or allow someone to challenge you to reach in for cocaine, heroin, marijuana, even tobacco or any other unlawful life threatening contraband knowing the horrible end results. Also, remember the fires of hell burn even hotter and forever. The drug users will then say, if John Doe or Jane Doe hadn't brought the burning garbage can here or there, they wouldn't have or been able to reach in, get burned, and destroy everything else they touch. "Please, please with ease take the leash off your own neck, before you finish hanging yourself."

CHAPTER 1

THE MAKING OF A COP

The making of this cop all began back in 1948 in Gary, Indiana. After leaving the hospital, I was brought to 1518 Tennessee St. As a little boy, I never learned to crawl, and when I was strong enough, I just started walking. I would only walk on a blanket and not the bare floor. One of the other things I remember as a little boy between 1948-1953 (1953 is when my three brothers and sister, Robert A., Barney M. Jr., Raymond L., Gloria J., and I left Indiana after our parents, Barney M. Allen Sr. and Essie M. Allen, divorced) is I use to remove the tops from the rear of our kitchen chairs and stuff my vegetables down into the chair posts to keep from eating them. I don't ever remember getting caught.

I also remember one day my dad took me to the live chicken market to get a chicken. The store workers caused the chicken to expire, de-feathered, wrapped and put it in a bag for the trip home. To this day, I believe that chicken was still alive in that bag next to me on the rear seat, and I was scared stiff (too scared to move or say anything), and I hoped my dad would hurry home. I use the term dad instead of father because I believe now that my only Father is my Heavenly Father. We also have a little notoriety in our family. My late grandfather's late brother (Dozier T. Allen, 1900-1999), owned and operated The First African American-owned gasoline station in Indiana. His son (Dozier T. Allen, Jr.) my cousin was a Trustee in Calumet Township, Lake County, Indiana for many years. He has a Councilman son in Gary, Indiana and also another son in the running for Mayor of Gary, Indiana (during the year of 2003). The then Congressman Danny K. Davis is my cousin's (Dozier) cousin.

My dad and mom never remarried after they were divorced. My mom had four more kids—Vicki E., Benson, Verna, and Paul—after we moved to Newark, N. J. Paul died before he left the hospital. My mom said my dad had one other child in Indiana, who we never met nor found out any other information about. When we left Indiana, we moved to Newark, N. J. in 1953. We lived at 19 Livingston Street which is where West Kinney St. School now sits. This is where my first run-in with crime occurred. I use to take illegal number slips for my mom upstairs to a neighbor not knowing at the time it was illegal. At that address is where I was also first robbed. My mom sent me to the store with a dollar to get a newspaper,*The Newark Star Ledger*. When two big tall guys ran up to me and said, "Give me your money or we'll kill you!" They forcefully took ninety-five cents from me, the change that was left over from the newspaper. This occurred around 1957-1958. This and other criminal activity began to strengthened my desire to become a cop. We moved from one apartment to the next one, on the average of once every 14 months between 1953 and 1966. We were extremely poor.

Livingston St. is the first street we lived on from 1953 to approximately 1955. It had only three rooms the six of us shared.

Mott St. was the second street we lived on from 1955 to approximately 1956. We moved in there with a new three piece furniture set. All of the furniture was repossessed and that winter we all ended up sleeping on a mattress on the floor, with bundles of clothes as cover/blankets. The mattress was what was left of the new furniture.

Wickcliffe St. was the third street we lived on from 1956 to approximately 1957.

West Kinney St. near Belmont Ave. now known as Irvine Turner Boulevard, behind a tavern, was the fourth street we lived on from 1957 to approximately 1958. Here is where I first learned a pinch of salt kept you from throwing up/vomiting. When we moved in, the bathroom toilet was backed up with human, and probably also animal solid, liquid waste, vomit or "Vom hit" and whatever else squatters/trespassers put in the filthy toilet. I, being the second oldest child, got elected to unstop and clean it. I did a thorough cleaning job and also got it to properly flush, and I didn't throw up. After getting evicted from that apartment, my mother, my brothers, Raymond and Barney Jr., and my sister Gloria all had to live in one of The Salvation Army's Shelters. My oldest brother (Robert) and myself had to live with a neighbor, it was either too many of us or we were too old for the shelter. I've always been grateful throughout the rest of my life for The Salvation Army's help. While on the city of Newark, N.J.'s. payroll as a police officer, I always donated a little something to them from my paycheck. We lived in that situation until we were able to find a suitable apartment for a mother with five children.

Prince St. was the fifth street we lived on from 1957 to approximately 1963. It had four rooms, the nine (three additional children) and sometimes eleven, which included my aunt and grandmother, of us shared. The hot water heater didn't work when we moved in and the wealthy landlord who owned a successful live fish market beneath us and another one elsewhere, never had it repaired nor replaced. It cost him less to have just cold water, especially with the use of a lot of cold water in his live fish market. We had to heat all of our bath water, whenever our electric and gas wasn't turned off. When the gas was turned

3

off, we made a charcoal fire in a five gallon can for heat during the winter. I believe the massive amounts of charcoal residue we inhaled, probably kept us healthy. When my last two sisters and brother were born, neither of them ever had a crib or a playpen. They, as newborns, slept in a soft blanket lined cardboard box on the kitchen table, where it was the warmest and away from the rodents.

Sherman Avenue was the sixth street we lived on from 1963 to approximately the end of that year.

Pennsylvania Avenue was the seventh street we lived on from 1963 to approximately 1964, where and when I also ended my newspaper route days. I then began employment as an usher in the old Branford Theater on Branford Place in Newark, N. J., where I was employed for 2 years.

Emmet St. was the eightth street we lived on, from 1964 to approximately the end of 1964 until we moved out, after it was condemned.

Emmet St. was close by (lucky for us) and became the ninth street we lived on from 1964 to approximately 1965. That was the street I began star gazing and where I met my eventual wife.

Hunterdon St. was the tenth street we lived on from 1965 to approximately the end of 1965.

Peshine Avenue was the eleventh street we lived on from 1965 to 1966 and beyond. I departed my beloved family (mother, brothers and sisters) in 1966 after graduating from high school and heded straight for induction into military service, the U.S.A.F. We had it extremely, extremely hard during my childhood. We often endured living without sufficient food, gas, electricity and clothing. We were evicted from most of the above addresses. Through it all, we remained drug and crime free, despite being poverty stricken (poor beyond the word poor) . My mother, who I love very much, did her very best to care for, teach, and guide us.

I became a *Newark Evening News* delivery paperboy in

1959 at the age of eleven. I lied and told the newspaper manager I was twelve. My oldest brother, Robert, was already delivering the same paper. I was a news delivery boy for five years. During that five years, I was robbed at least four times, twice by the same person. He also robbed my oldest brother. The last time this person robbed me, he followed me along my entire paper route ducking in and out of hallways. My mother's boyfriend, being aware of the earlier robbery, came along with me on my money collection day to try and prevent another robbery. I had three houses left to deliver to and we were across the street from where I lived so my stepdad, which is how we referred to him, said he was leaving. He stated, prior to leaving, "Aw that m'f (my friend) ain't coming." He closed his knife he had open in his hand, undetected, placed it in his pocket, and left. I had two stops left. On the second stop, the thief appeared in the hallway brandishing a butcher knife. He took all of my collection money and fled on foot. I ran across the street into my house screaming, "He robbed me, he robbed me." My stepdad was in complete shock, he couldn't believe the guy followed us over the entire route and stayed out of sight. The police were eventually called and the thief was later arrested. The detectives brought the suspect to us in their unmarked police car for identification.

When they asked me if it was him, McGhee winked for me to say "no."

I said, "Yes that's him." We never found out what happened in court.

He later showed up at my 7th Avenue Junior High School with about five to seven guys. I believe they were looking for me and my brother. I also believe I saw them before they saw me, and I got in the wind (ran). The first and only time I looked back, I didn't see the school nor them, I didn't have any other contact with him after that as a teen. The only other time I saw and recognized him was after I became a police officer and that chance meeting occurred in the old A&P Supermarket on Spruce

St. He and a female were at the end of a checkout counter. The female called out his name. I was working part time as a police officer in the A&P. Then, and for the rest of my life, whenever I heard that name, I paid attention. So I turned, looked, and thirty years went by in a flash. I said, "I don't believe it. That's that jerk off." All I did at that point was etch a picture of his face in my memory, and I haven't seen him since.

Also, during that time period as a young teen, I remember being in a crowd watching a fight one evening on South Orange Avenue between Prince Street and Rankin Street. The fight involved a neighborhood adult and some neighborhood teens. I knew the adult male very well. I use to fight with his two sons all the time. On this evening the adult man had a butcher knife menacingly waving it, keeping the four to five teens at bay. He then looked past them and for some reason came after me with the knife in a stabbing position. I ran east on South Orange Avenue, making a right turn south on Prince Street toward my house. I ran up the front steps thinking he would back off. He continued after me. I stepped up the pace and barely increased enough distance between us as he swung the knife toward my back in a slashing motion and, luckily for me, missed. I aborted my attempt to run into the house. Instead, I jumped off the right side of the porch and disappeared very quickly into the crowd. The adult man then turned around in a crazed motion, apparently looking for someone else to attack. The crowd, disturbed over the fact I was almost cut and/or killed for nothing, urged a known older teen onlooker who had been training daily at the then *Dukers Athletic Club*, boxing club, to take on the adult man, who at this time had turned into a mad man. *The Duker's A.C.* trainee approached the mad man in a circling motion and threw a punch that was called a haymaker, a wild overhand swing to the head, as if you're pitching hay, causing the mad man to lose his balance. The trainee then moved in closer and hit him with what was called the Jamesburg Roll, first learned in *The Jamesburg Reformatory*. It's a continuous rolling flurry of punches to all parts of the upper body in close quarters, not noted for power, but for the speed of the punches and psychological effect. If you're hit with it unexpectedly you usually ran or lost the fight. The mad man ended up doing both. The Jamesburg Roll dislodged the knife from the mad man's hand and caused him to hit the ground back first. Someone in the crowd picked up the knife. The madman picked himself up and then picked up a nearby 2x4. He began waving it menacingly at the crowd, keeping them at bay. An uninvolved and unconcerned man, who had just gotten off the bus walked out in the street, to avoid and get pass the crowd. He got too close to the madman and was smashed across his head with the 2x4 causing it to break in half. The blow almost knocked him out. He was dazed, stumbling, wouldn't stay down and just kept trying to leave. The crowd began jumping on cars, hollering, and shouting for the man to get with (fight him) the mad man. The still dazed and confused man just staggered away. The madman wildly looked around and as the crowd grew, took his only and very smart opportunity to flee into the nearby firehouse. He remained with the firemen/firefighters who guarded the entrance. The firemen during those times were as respected as police officers. The madman was probably in the firehouse laughing— "He, he, ha, ha. I couldn't catch those jitter bugs or that skinny sleepy eyed boy. That *Duker's A. C.* boy was good, but I knocked the s— out of that other jitter bug. …he, he, ha, ha." The police never did respond, if they were even called. After the crowd filtered out, the madman eventually booked (left) and eased back to Rankin St. He eventually died after he and his family moved to the south ward section of Newark, N.J. Ironically the madman's two sons, who I fought with almost everyday, spent most of their adult life in and out of prison for various crimes. One son did time in jail for a homicide. He shot a man in the back of the head after the man snatched his mother's purse. He eventually ran down on the man, ordered him into his car, and as the man bent down to get in the car, he was shot. The other son did time for bank robberies. He was known as "The Jogging Bandit." He would rob banks and jog from the scene in colorful jogging suits. Some of his jogging suits, Mr. Charles could identify from his private jet at altitude.

The third robbery was committed while I was delivering newspapers, by a male known as one of the Gilmore brothers. It occurred on Springfield Avenue nearBroome Street at knife point. He was later shot gun killed for robbing an illegal numbers runner, which was a no-no then and today.

The fourth robbery occurred as I was again delivering newspapers. I was on Springfield Ave., where it joins South Orange Ave. An older man approached me and asked me to help him get some boxes from his car, which he said was parked right around the corner. I agreed. I made sure he led the way, and I walked slightly behind him. I also continued to look back, watching out for the rear end double team. I apparently looked back one time too often. The man turned and charged me. Being proud of my foot speed, I wasn't worried because I knew I could outrun him. As I pivoted to take off, I tripped and fell. I only saw that on television. It never happened to me before. The man jumped on me and put one of those banana knives to my throat and said, "I ought to kill you." He ransacked my pockets while I was still on the ground, took what I had, got up and booked. The police were never called for that robbery, the first one or the third one, which was the way things were back then. All those incidents and others continued to fuel my desire to become a cop.

I left the newspaper business and became an usher at the pay rate of 55 cents an hour, I eventually managed to reach 75 cents an hour before I left. I was employed in the old Branford Theatre on Branford Place for two years, until I graduated from South Side High School and entered the military in 1966. I didn't have too many problems in high school. I was one of the (S) boys (shy, skinny, to the tune of 6' 2", 115 to 125 pounds light and smart). I was too skinny to breath hard, and I would often look down at my chest and could see my heart beat. I always said, without any other choices YOU HAVE TO BE THIN TO WIN and FAT IS NOT WHERE IT'S AT.

When I was in grammar school not only was I thin, I had a sleepy looking appearance. I was nicknamed "Sleepy" and some not so wise guys that used to judg with me stretched it to "Sleepy Joe, Sleepy Joe Roach, and Sleepy Joe Cocker Roach."

I joined the U.S.A.F on June 28, 1966, six days after high school graduation. As you now see and read, I was in a hurry to leave town. My Air Force basic training was completed at Lackland A.F.B in Texas. My aircraft mechanic training was completed at Chanute A. F. B. in Illinois. After leaving there I went to visit my dad in Gary, Indiana. This was the first time I had seen him in twelve years.

After leaving his house, I experienced my first remembered incident of racism. During the Vietnam War, I got on a bus in full military uniform, and I sat next to a white older lady in one of the few vacant seats. She angrily jumped up, mumbling, and changed seats. An adult male, who I believed to be her son, tried to make her sit down next to me, but she wasn't having it. He appeared to be as embarrassed as I was although I quickly got over it.

The U.S.A.F. ordered me to Ellsworth A.F.B. in South Dakota, assigned to the 28th Bomb Wing where I remained until 1970. While there, I spent six months in Southeast Asia, where I went on refueling missions as a crew chief. I remember once while stationed at Ellsworth A.F.B., I was walking through a field and some birds flew down toward me in attack formation. When they got too close, I ducked, picked up a tree limb, and waved them off. When I got to my barracks and relayed what had happened to one of my G. I. friends, he replied, "They (the birds) thought you were something dead cause you walk so slow," I agreed but I didn't let him know.

Before I wasdischarged from the U.S.A.F. active duty, I took and passed The N.Y.C. Police Department's police examination, otherwise I wouldn't have gotten out of the military. After I was discharged and while waiting for the N.Y.C. Police Dept. to call me, during the last days of June, 1970. I took and passed The Newark, N.J. Police Department's civil service test. I came out number eleven out of the thousand or more applicants that tested. The long awaited making of a cop was in its beginning stages.

During my otherwise smooth initial police department investigation, this occurrence stands out. My investigator wanted to know why I was wearing a trench rain coat on a rainy summer day, which was the day I had to report to him. He wasn't aware I had spent most of the last four years, stationed in very cold Rapid City, S.D. and was accustomed to wearing some type of outer garment. He had me remove it and proceeded to check both of my arms for drug involvement and found nothing. I honestly believe if I hadn't been in the military during The Vietnam War, and I hadn't scored as high as I did on the police exam, my investigator would've found a way to deny my entrance onto the police department. Back then, applicants were denied the job if they lived with a male or female and weren't married to the person, if family members were incarcerated, if you had a child and weren't married to the child's parent, or if you had a bad driving record, among many other things.

In August of 1970, I got married and eventually divorced. That union produced a lovely daughter, Kimberly, and two handsome sons, Richard II, Radell I. I later on had three lovely daughters, Kiva, Denita, Brittany, and one stepdaughter, Courtney. I've also been blessed with five grandchildren, Richard II, Imari, Davion, Ty'Kala, and Radell Jr..

In 1971, I joined The U.S.A.F. Reserves at McGuire A.F.B. I started as an aircraft mechanic, then eventually became a flight engineer, a pilot's technical advisor, until I retired on January 15, 1996. My military service totaled 28½ years, which included ten months of activation during the Desert Shield/Storm War. My military tours were mostly pleasant. Although there were times while in the reserves I was suspected of drug use, I didn't feel that way while on active duty. While in the reserves, the 335th Military Airlift Squadron, I was once told by my first sergeant, I would be randomly drug tested after lunch.

I said, "Okay, when did they pull names?"

He said, "They didn't, but your name will get pulled," and he walked away.

I also walked away mumbling, "What kind of random drawing is that?"

I believe they were hoping I would sign out after lunch and leave avoiding the drug test. I reported back after lunch and took the rigged drug test and eventually passed that one and the later ones because there was never a reason for me not to pass.

There was another time in Saudi Arabia, during the Desert Storm War, I left a tent where movies were being shown. I left in the middle of the movie leaving the other crew members behind because I was returning to my crew's tent. In the interim, I headed toward the outhouse tent, where the urinals and toilets were located, to take a dump. I, with the help of my several years of police skills, felt as if I was being followed. I looked slightly to my right rear without turning my head completely around, I saw one of our aircraft pilots following me. After being initially shocked and disbelieving, I repeated my glance a second time. This time the pilot had slightly crouched while still following me, in an attempt to hide from my view. I continued to walk as if I didn't see him I said, "Okay, if he wants to follow me to the dump house, shower and to my sleeping bag which was in a tent, he's welcome." I never did look back again to see if he continued to follow me any further. I believe then and now I was followed because he thought I was going somewhere to use drugs, especially after he observed me leave the movie tent with the other crew members still there. I didn't have any further cat and mouse scenarios with that pilot, but I did have another suspicion of drug use encounter with another crew member. This incident occurred in flight abroad a C (Cargo) 141B Aircraft somewhere between 29 and 41 thousand feet, involving a loadmaster, responsible for loading the aircraft, and myself. I left the flight station where my station as a flight engineer was located and went down into the cargo compartment to use the relief/rest room. After I finished discharging my waste water, I flushed the toilet and washed my hands. I pushed the relief room door open, which had been closed but not locked, and it smashed the loadmaster on the side of his head and face. He was apparently listening with the side of his face and head up against the door. After the door hit him, he embarrassingly walked away without saying anything and without touching his face or head. He acted as if what just happened didn't happen. He didn't even wait for me to apologize. I guess he said to himself, "NO APOLOGY NEEDED. I WAS JUST LISTENING FOR DRUG USE SOUNDS. IF YOU HAD LOCKED THE DOOR, ASSHOLE, THAT WOULD'VE BEEN MY CUE TO MOVE MY HEAD AND FACE ONCE YOU UNLOCKED IT. BESIDES THAT MY EYE GLASSES ARE OKAY."

What makes me so sure he was listening at the door is when I initially opened the door, he appeared to be just starting to lean toward the door and he observed me go into the relief room. I've had to deal with the suspicion of drug use all of my adult life. I don't smoke or use drugs and never did. Which brings to memory the saying, "Don't Judge A Book By Its Cover" is fashionable and now that drugs have become deliberately fashionable. I have to deal with constant drug use suspicion. Females never had a problem with me being deliberate and never in a hurry. I honestly believe because of The Love of God and my deliberate actions I'm still here. Speaking of looking/being calm and laid back, I completed a required military reserves annual flight physical at McGuire A.F.B., and my medical records were left with the flight surgeon, to be reviewed and signed which was required for me to remain on flying status. While the flight surgeon was reviewing them, he matched my age, sex, height, weight, and whatever other parameters he used against my blood pressure and pulse rate results. He immediately thought his staff was playing a trick on him, by putting together a dummy medical record and hoping he would sign it. He said, "The numbers from this blood pressure and pulse rate would indicate this person is dead." So the quick thinking surgeon figured he'll get a jump on his staff and call my supervisor and find out if I existed. After my supervisor, a MSGT/E7-MasterSergeant/Enlisted Seven, confirmed, while laughing with the entire office, I was a very real person. The flight surgeon, an officer, ordered my supervisor to have me respond back to the hospital and see him personally and for me to jog there, if I was indeed a for real person. I got the quite hilarious message and with no choice I responded back, I briskly walked part of the way to help stimulate my blood pressure. The flight surgeon redid the necessary tests and eventually agreed I was a living being, even without high blood pressure. My 28½ years of active and reserve military duty were mostly good and memorable years. I served all of my military reserve duty while I was employed as a City of Newark patrolman (later changed to police officer). My entire career began and ended as a police officer. My promotional examinations I took and passed, but I was too far down on the list to get promoted. One later promotional test I took, I passed the written portion and was told I failed the oral portion. This was another case, I believe, I was being suspected of drug use. I honestly believe the oral assessment examiner failed me because he didn't know me, and I probably looked high to him. I had a feeling he was going to fail me when I walked into the room, looked at him and sat down. Instead of assessing my answers, he assessed my motions and unknowing to him my natural facial expressions. I worked my part time security job the night before, which didn't help. I could've appealed that examiner's decision, like a lot of other officers did and had his decision reversed. I felt in my heart if I had to appeal or cheat, I didn't want to be a supervisor. Oh, by the way, some officers did cheat to get promoted. I once heard a sergeant tell a lieutenant, "Hey, Lieutenant, I'm taking the lieutenant's test soon, and I got a copy of the test right here. My problem is I still have to pick the right answers and remember them." The lieutenant nodded with a facial expression of "yeah, that's your problem." The sergeant eventually put the unauthorized test away and began another conversation.

STAY INTERESTED

Question: What do you call a deer that can't see?

Answer: ?
No Idea—
Then think about it, while you continue reading:

OFFICERS MUST ARM THEMSELVES WITH THE LOVE OF GOD

All police officers whether they're on the streets, in the prisons, in the courts or wherever they're assigned must be prepared to confront every confrontation armed with The Love of God. The must also learn to freely sense and feel only the fear of God, fearing no one else or any incident they may confront. A lot of law breakers today are more disrespectful and physical in their appearances, and overt actions than ever before. Some of our prisons have allowed a lot of our incorrigible lawbreakers to return to society even more physical and menacing in appearance. Some of them now have the physical and mental skills learned in prison to commit crimes without using a gun. Thus making a police officer's job on the outside even more demanding, difficult, and stressful. Police officers are constantly reminded to use only the minimum force required to disarm a suspect or make a situation safe. God's Love is the greatest force that will ever be, it can be attained and applied in every situation by praying, trusting in God, and asking Him to guide our every action. Always remember that police officers are looked upon as the last ones in the line continuing to help our children keep their caps on straight and follow their brims. We are also looked upon as not to fail, where our families, schools and churches have sometimes failed to tow the line to the end. We as parents have sometimes, allowed our children to turn their caps sideways, backwards, and followed their brims in the wrong directions. Police officers with all they're entrusted with, are also looked upon to redirect our misdirected loved ones.

MY FIRST PARTNER

My first partner was shot and killed in an off duty incident. His wife was also shot and killed along with another person. The East Orange, N.J. police were on the scene and involved. He was a good cop, good boxer for his size (five feet seven inches tall, one hundred seventy five-one hundred eighty pounds light) and an exceptional basketball player (no disrespect Brit). We use to play basketball and box in the old police academy on 18th Avenue. He told me once, in all his boxing days, "You hit me with the hardest left hand I've ever been hit with," by me being a southpaw, I didn't really have a right hand. We remained close friends even after we split as police partners. He became a decoy detective, and I remained in the South District Police Station where I served more than thirty and a half years. We were involved in a lot of good police actions, but back in 1971 supervisors didn't commend you in writing for excellent police work unless you damn near begged them. I was on the department a number of years before I got my first commendation award because I never asked anyone to recognize my work. I was the same officer in 1971 as I was in 2001, just a little heavier, going from one hundred forty to two hundred pounds; more wiser and a little more apprehensive, but with the same work ethic. While in the Newark, New Jersey

Police Academy, things went relatively smooth with the exception of the following incident:

One Monday morning, one of our instructors said, "Men, the health department lab personnel called us and said they lost six of you all's urine specimens. The following names will have to respond immediately to the lab and resubmit urine specimens." I knew right then and there my name would be called and it was, along with five other "bulls—" names because it was me they wanted. We resubmitted the specimens and heard nothing further. My classmate and eventual first steady partner took exception to the lie we were told. He questioned one of our instructors as to when the investigating would cease. He didn't receive a definite answer. He also knew they were after me merely based on my God given demeanor.

MISSED PARTNER

This particular evening my new partner (a.k.a. Lenny) and I had, with probable cause, stopped a suspect. The suspect was a short male, chiseled physique with good strong hands. The subject somehow got on why he was hanging around a drug area and moved to his insisting that we were both punks. He narrowed it down to my partner being the bigger punk. My partner was six feet tall, two hundred and forty pounds, ex-correctional officer, ex-boxer with good hands and if Lenny shot him one, one-on-one, he would prove it to him and I could wait in line to get mine. Lenny, against the rules, shot him the one, and with one punch dropped him with a powerful short right hand upper cut to the body. The suspect appeared to be looking for a left hand jab as he was bopping and weaving while moving toward Lenny. The suspect slowly got up and said, "Damn, all your strength is upstairs."

Lenny said, "Yeah, all two hundred and forty pounds."

The suspect peeped (caught) me laughing and said, "Sleepy,

laugh while you can. If I had shot you the one first, you would've been in the hospital right about now."

I said, "Yeah you're right, I would've been in the hospital, right about now up under your bed with my foot still stuck in your rear end."

He said, "All right, Sleep, you got that off, but check this out. Now, now, listen to what I'm saying. Me and you're going to still get our one off some other time, and I guarantee the script will flip."

I replied with, "You and your script flipping tail can meet me at Hawthorne Avenue and Elizabeth Avenue (near the local eatery), and like that real old song 'Any Day Now.' I just might have you flipping burgers. Now put that in your script and watch me act." With that reply, the suspect dropped, shook his head, and stepped off.

Lenny was a big strong officer, no foot speed, good basketball player. He always spoke well of me to his family. Some of my most memorable drug arrests occurred while we were partners. When he died, he left behind a lovely wife, and we became close friends. She always believed his death was planned by some of his so called in-the-shadows-moving associates.

QUEEN LATIFAH'S FATHER

My early days as a police officer were mostly good. I had the opportunity to work with several different patrolmen during 1971. One of them being Patrolman/Police Officer L. O., a.k.a. Lance, who was Queen Latifah's father. When discussing how he met her mother, he stated, "I used to ride my bike (motorcycle) to and from Washington, D. C. to see this girl. She got pregnant. I wasn't going back, and her family came looking for me, and I had to get married."

I said, "Yeah, like a shot gun wedding." He laughed. He would often imitate playing different instruments to strangers after conversations would lead to music. Those strangers would leave, believing he had and could play those instruments. He would later confess that in reality he couldn't and that it was all part of his gift. I told him at one time I was thinking about getting into the life insurance business. He said, "Naw, that ain't you. You need the gift of gab like me." Which is probably one of the reasons his daughter became so successful with her gifts. He said at one time he belonged to a gang as a teen out of the north ward called The Four Horsemen and whenever he or another member got into trouble with the police, they would grab some other kid/s and make them confess to whatever happened. He also stated his looks were the result of his grandfather or father being Indian.

One evening while on patrol, Lance and a street suspect got into a discussion about boxing. Lance had exceptional hand skills. As the discussion became heated, the suspect told Lance, "I think I can get next to you (meaning beat his behind)."

Lance replied, "How much do you weigh?"

The suspect answered, "One hundred and sixty-five pounds."

Lance said, "I hope you got all of that one hundred and sixty-five pounds in one arm before you come here." As the suspect stuttered for a reply, Lance peeled off in the police car laughing. He added, "I don't even spar with jokers under two hundred pounds plus," that don't hit hard."

I said, "Yeah," while laughing with all of my one hundred and forty-one hundred fifty pounds."

Lance eventually left the department. When I saw him again, he was wearing a carpenter's tool belt loaded with tools and said he was in the home remodeling business. The last time I saw him, he stated he was living in Virginia and that he might be getting involved with his daughter's security detail. He further added his daughter was coming to Newark, N.J., and that he would be given the key to the city. I don't know if that ever came about. No matter what, Lance was The South District Police Precinct's coolest and one of the most popular cops in the seventies. When you look at his daughter you're looking at young Lance.

OFFICER'S TRUST

Most of the police officers during my era were professional and honest. There were some, as with any other profession, that couldn't be trusted. There were officers who gave out your home address and phone numbers to known drug dealers. I would regularly put incorrect addresses on my police station emergency recall cards. I would list my pager and/or cell telephone number as my home telephone number to protect my family. An intelligent squad detective once told me, it was a $35,000 hit out on my partner at the time and myself. We were known as Buck and The Preacher in the street. My partner was also a minister. The detective further stated, "An officer assigned to your police station has already given out your addresses." Mine was fictitious, so I wasn't worried. The junkie hit man died from AIDS before earning his pay. This was all later confirmed during a conversation with a drug dealer. He was trying to clear his name, as being one of the financiers. Police officers got suspended, fired, and/or arrested for unlawful drug involvement. We must remember they are from and part of an under-the-influence society. When the Newark Police Department assumed an officer, they didn't and couldn't lay aside the citizen and/or where he/she came from.

There was this incident that occurred, when I was working part time on Elizabeth Ave. An off duty police officer walked in the popular establishment and placed his order. I walked over to him offering a raffle ticket for sale. He began nervously, shaking, trembling and he started to slowly back up as if he was going to step off. I believe he thought I was going to frisk him. I stopped walking toward him and said to myself, "Damn, is he holding or what?" After collecting his composure, he began to realize why I walked over to him. He looked at the raffle book in my hand and said, "Yeah, okay, how many you want me to buy?"

I said, "One is cool."

He gave me the $5.00, got his ticket stub, his order and then stepped off. He eventually got stepped on and booted from the police department.

The same above police officer, prior to getting the boot, was working in uniform one day in a marked police vehicle as the driver. He was also sipping on a cool one, a can of beer—a gross no, no. Apparently he was so into the brew, he forgot he wasn't the only moving vehicle on the road. As a result, he caused a motor vehicle accident with another vehicle, splashing his beer all over his uniform, wasting very good brew. He pulled the police vehicle over, threw the remaining can of beer out his window, which was against his beer drinking ethics. He quickly tried to wipe as much beer off his uniform, that he could. He finally exited his vehicle, after learning his embarrassed partner was uninjured. The previously damaged police vehicle, upon inspection, appeared not to have any new damage. He approached the female driver of the other involved vehicle. She indicated she was uninjured, but her vehicle was smashed up, not pretty bad but awfully bad. The officer, while trying to look as professional as possible, except for his beer spattered uniform and breath, continued to look over the nervous female's vehicle, while mumbling and stalling for a good explanation. Despite his drinking, he was still looking, walking, and talking good after probably throwing down several battery charged breath mints. He then said to the female, "We have a problem."

She replied, "Yes officer, I have problems. I don't have a driver's license. I just brought this car. It's not registered or insured."

Now, the officer's light footed feeling of guilt appeared to shift from his conscience to the female motorist's admission of "Her problem." He acknowledged that approved shift by saying, "Yes madam, YOU Do Have Some Serious Problems. Being that I'm feeling good here today, here's what can happen and you can make it happen. To avoid writing you several summonses, towing your vehicle and probably arresting you on any open bench warrants that we all have (while smiling), let's let this little mishap disappear. You make a telephone call, have your ride towed to wherever and since no one is injured, I can continue on with some more pressing police business." The relieved female happily agreed and the alcoholic police officer walked and then drove away, smiling. The maladjusted officer was eventually permanently sent on his way to continue his wayward ways and sad days.

Another off duty police officer during another incident approached my partner and myself while we were working in uniform on Avon Ave. and Hunterdon St. I was searching a friend of the off duty officer's. The officer called out, "Fam/family. He's all right. I know him."

I said, "Okay, but he's under arrest." The off duty officer didn't know, I had already recovered drugs, cocaine.

The off duty officer said, "For what? He ain't done nothing. He's been with me all day."

After I showed him the drugs, he shut up while sipping from his glass and stumbling back into the bar with his glass of liquor, cat hit as my maternal grandmother called it. That officer was lucky, stumbled around and out the way long enough, and got to retire from the police department.

Here's another incident involving a police officer, who left the department for personal reasons:

I was assigned to work with him for that evening in a marked police vehicle. We eventually approached a suspect, who we had reason to believe was selling drugs on the SW corner of Bergen St. and Hawthorne Ave. After we were satisfied, we approached the suspect arrested and wristcuffed him. After I wristcuffed him, I turned to hand him over to my partner, so I could retrieve the stash/drugs. My partner turned his back to us. He apparently knew the prisoner and didn't want his face seen. I had to place the prisoner in our police vehicle and then retrieve the drugs. Before my partner got into our vehicle, he took out a pair of dark sunglasses, put them on and drove us to the police station. He remained in our police vehicle while I escorted the prisoner into the police station and completed all of the arrest paper work. My partner, for that evening, had already been suspected of unlawful drug involvement. I learned, he had previously purchased drugs from our prisoner and didn't want him to see his face. He learned that unlawful drug use and police work didn't and won't work.

Another incident involving a police officer who partnered with me for the evening occurred while we were on patrol in a marked police vehicle on Clinton Ave. between Bergen St. and Chadwick Ave. We observed suspected drug activity. The two involved suspects booked (ran) into a store, and we ran in after them. The suspect I caught was apprehended while trying to discard drugs, resulting in his being arrested. The second suspect my partner caught was frisked, advised, and sent on his way (s.o.w.). My partner said he was clean, so we transported the one prisoner to he South District Police Station. Once there, the prisoner called out to me and whispered, "Yo, Buck, how come y'all let my boy walk? He had the exact same s— I had."

I said, "Look, I caught you, I didn't catch or check him."

He said, "That's horse s—, boss man gave us the same s— to clock."

I continued with the paper work. My partner had gone to the bowel movement room. I never called it a bath room because there's no shower or tub. When he returned, he had to turn deaf ears to the verbal salads (profanity) he received from the prisoner. As of this writing, that officer did have problems and is still presently on the department. He had a brother, a lieutenant, who wasn't so lucky. Believe it or not, most police officers are good and honest. Unfortunately, people like to read about the corrupt, bad ones.

This short incident didn't even make it into the police station. I pulled in front with a suspect in the rear to verify a warrant. I was working as a one man patrol unit, so I had to run into the station to call in a verification warrant check. So I asked another officer, a one man unit parked in front of the station, to watch my suspect while I went in to use the phone. Some desk lieutenants didn't want you to bring in prisoners without prior verification of any warrants. When I came out of the station, the other officer and the suspect were gone. I won't say if the suspect came up wanted and I care, even less about the officer's whereabouts. It's obvious he didn't care, how I got out of that situation. The suspect turned out to be an indebted friend of his.

Is It True?

Professional, neatly pressed uniformed, highly polished footwear and facially groomed officers could portray a soft image, in some of our too much tough neighborhoods. What about the above appearances on an officer, with the exception of the facial grooming. Replacing it with a little unshaven facial growth, to possibly toughen an officer's facial image.

Let's read and look at the following true incident:

Two young men were wilding on a street corner, when they observed two police officers on foot patrol, approaching from the other side of the street. One of the young men said, "Word that big cop looks mad as hell, and as if he hasn't shaved in a day or two." The second young man said, "Yeah how 'bout in three or four days, he look seious/serious as hell, let's bounce/move on." The police officer's tough looking facial grooming moved the two young men on, without too much effort or the officers even being aware of what had happen. Wilding could include anything from funning, unlawful drug activity, gang banging, a small mini riot in its beginning stages and to hitting somebody up/shooting them. A police officer's presence and unshaved face handled that wilding incident, also the officer may have been waiting for a sale on shavers at one of the local inexpensive grocery stores. Uniformed **t**ough **o**fficers **u**nfortunately **g**et **h**eckled by their supervisors, when they don't shave and won't in the long or short run benefit, from that get tough (**t**oo bad **o**fficers **u** **g**uys **h**ave to shave) look.

DAD AND MOM

I truly thank Our Lord for my parents
I also truly thank Him for their parents

Without them, there would be no me
Without them, there would be no children to call my own

If I continued to go back into time and thank Him for all
    births connected to me
All thanks would lead back to Our Lord, The Father of Life
Which is where, hopefully all of our traveled roads will also
    lead us, back to Our Lord in Heaven

Which is why I truly believe in thanking Our Lord for being
    Who He is and what He has done for all of humanity
Without Our Lord being Who He is, there would be no
    Love, Hope, Faith or any Peace, whatsoever or forever

I will always be thankful to my late dad (Barney M. Allen,
    Sr.) and my mother (Essie M. Allen), for their parts in
    bringing me into this world, along with all of my brothers
    and sisters

THANK YOU LORD, Dad and Mom

DEDICATED TO THE NEWARK NEW JERSEY'S FINEST FEMALE OFFICERS EVER IN BLUE

Hello to all the ladies in your true blue
The so few, but sure in their endeavors, of true blue
True to God, their families, themselves and the N.P.D.
Fearing God and protecting the lives of all citizens for the
    N.P.D.
So beautiful and true in blue,
Looking like a bundle of roses in blue
So feminine true in everything you do.
There's no P.D. to compare you to.
Say hi to the true, still remaining within the true blue
Say bye to the few, who jumped ship and landed in the blue
Since I left you all, I'm feeling a little blue
But while I'm gone, maintain that all spirited true blue
Set your goals way beyond the sky blue
Set and maintain your high standards until the place turns
    blue.
With true blue love,
True blue love,
True blue,
Ru blue,
Ru,

Richard L. Allen, retired, yes I am

A BEAUTIFUL WOMAN

God's beautiful gift to man,

And all of the added beautiful pleasures in having a good woman.

All so different in how they're so softly and beautifully curved in this round world of man's

So pleasing in how some of them talk with their walk, while controlling the eyes of most girl watching men

Their beautifully manicured toe nails and finger nails, may just help nail an artistic looking male

Have you ever noticed a woman's beautifully arched lips, which were probably made for a keen eyed gentleman

What about their beautiful eyes which are the revealing and heart breaking mirrors of their hearts, if you look closely, you may be able to see, if there's someone else claiming her as his.

Even though, most of the time they use their hearts, instead of their heads, but

They're still all in body and soul, our lovely women, which is pleasing to their

Masculine males

A woman's hair is her glory and she is his glory, in the eyes and hands of her only man

To all of the men reading this page of the book, turn and kiss something beautiful on your lovely lady if she's next to you, and don't forget to return to finish what you started. (This book!)

And all women will always be beautiful women. I dedicate this poem to every beautiful woman who reads it

Please read this book in a smoke free environment—

"Where there's smoke, there's fire and that fire maybe burning up your lungs"

When smoke is entering your airspace, your sense of sight and smell usually warns you there's something burning under control or out of control. You then take the necessary and proper actions to smoke free your airspace. When your body and all of your senses identify self induced sickarette (a.k.a. cigarette) smoke entering your body's airspace. We should take the proper life saving action and quit. Our mouths have always been considered as the one body part we lack complete control of and will probably never control. Some of us talk and eat too much, and of course if we smoke at all, it's much too much. Sickarette smelling breath, stained teeth, burned lips and fingers, short winded, soot coated lungs, cancer, other ailments and eventually an untimely death are the possible rewards from smoking sickarettes. Give me a break and I don't mean a sickarette break. Get on the real side of a sickarette, after you've thrown it down and stomped it out of you life forever.

Smoking is not a
And breathing in second hand smoke is not a
Joking matter
It's a matter
Of life and death
And none sickarette smelling breath
There'll be no smoking in Heaven
So why should you smoke in your presence haven
There'll be plenty of smoking and fires in hell
Don't you know and if you do I can't tell
Smoke free
Is to breath free
Sickarette smoking is a defect
That creates a too much birth and after a birth defect

Sickarette smoking is a hard earned monetary risk,
Placing your God Given Good Health at risk.
Sickarette tobacco has its place in history,
Hopefully it won't cause you to become history
No sickarette in your hand
Is just as good as the whole pack being thrown away in a
    bush by the same hand.
The U.S.A.F. just prior to a sickarette break use to say if u
    got'em light'em up.
What they were really saying was if u got'em darken'em
    lungs up.
Sickarette tobacco products can cause expensive damages
And also some extensive damages.
It's up to you to smoke sickarettes with a chance to suffer
Or not to smoke sickarettes and not be known as a puffer
Why would you spend hard earned money on sickarettes
    to eventually suffer
When it's free not to ever become a puffer?
Sickarette smoking is a very bad deal.
I'm being For Real
And this is the real deal.
Sickars (a.k.a. cig-ars) has a masculine ending
Sickarettes (a.k.a. cig-a-rettes) has a feminine ending

So all of you so called males walking around with a pack or
two of sickarettes in your pockets. Are you all wearing panties,
boxers, briefs or what. All of you females walking around with
sickars in your pockets, bags or where ever. What are you all
wearing, do you smoke what you are, as in **sick**arettes. "Thank
you very much for not smoking now and hopefully forever"

DURING READER'S INTERMISSION

SOME WORDS TO THE MUCH TOO WISE
TO REMIND THE NOT SO WISE

DON'T DRINK AND DRIVE!

And if you do drive after consuming strong drink,
You may end up driving on the brink
And off or into some road side dink.
You may someday want to see your lovely lady in a mink
And not elephants in the pink.
You may want to stay sober and continue to think
And help maintain that strong family link.
You may also want to return home to the wife and kids with
    a wink
And not bent over running straight to the sink.
You may report a dwi and not be considered a fink
And I'll put that on paper and in ink.
You may want to drive hard, then take it to the hockey rink.

"For the real face off"
"And not an accidental DWI face off."

CHAPTER II

THREE OF MY MILITARY
RESERVES PARTNERS

This following incident was one of the many motor vehicle pursuits, the police officer known as the Rev and I (a.k.a. Buck) were involved in as recent police partners. We, with probable cause, attempted to pull over a motor vehicle, traveling east on Clinton Avenue. They turned north on Washington Street, which was a one way street at the time going northbound. The driver of the pursued vehicle began accelerating, after getting a good distance in front of us. He then hit his brakes and attempted to slow down to make a tight left turn onto a very narrow side street, which isn't there anymore. It was very hard to get onto that extremely narrow street even while being stopped and perpendicular to it. This driver, now a suspect, attempted that turn on a ninety degree angle on the right front wheel, speeding in what appeared to be one of those extra long Cadillacs. Nevertheless, the suspect, along with a female front seat passenger, attempted the improbable high speed turn, which no one could have negotiated. What partially helped prevent the attempted completion of the turn was a very large old sturdy tree, which bordered and appeared to guard the entrance to the narrow street. The Cadillac impacted the tree and crumbled. The female passenger, who we later discovered was pregnant, was immediately and cleanly ejected from the right front passenger's door of the vehicle as all the doors flew open. She landed in the middle of Washington St., face up, which was lucky for her unborn baby. The female's large butt cushioned her airborne crash to the pavement. The driver miraculously remained in the vehicle, but hurriedly exited and hit the ground, running northbound on Washington St. During his fright flight he ran up on his pregnant girlfriend lying in the street and in stride, leaped over her outstretched body and continued booking without a suggestion of a pause. My partner and I were initially stunned and speechless, thinking the pregnant passenger might be dead. My partner rushed over to her to render whatever medical assistance he had available. He was a medical technician at one time in The United States Air Force Reserves at McGuire Air Force Base in Wrightstown, New Jersey). The suspect appeared to have accelerated as he leaped over his pregnant girlfriend. I guess he figured the car was smashed all to hell, his girlfriend might be d.o.a (dead on arrival), it was time to be outta there, and he continued hauling butt northbound. In the meantime, I put my leather soles in the weather, running after him. I eventually caught up to him and brought him down like a feather. It turned out he wasn't hauling as much butt as we initially figured. He turned out kind of on-the-light behind side. After wristcuffing him and walking him back to the scene, he tearfully and fearfully begged me to let him see his pregnant girl to make sure she was all right. She was being attended to by medical technicians from the arriving ambulance. I denied his request, and I asked him, "Why didn't look down to ask her that while you were leaping over her? You didn't say, 'Baby, you al'ight? I'm outta here for right now. I'll git back to you in a few.'" He didn't answer me, and his tears turned into a rolling stream, but couldn't wash away the thought of his leaving his pregnant girlfriend stretched out in the street on her butt. He turned out to be a bus driver walking a tight rope with his employer. With no motor vehicle insurance on his unregistered vehicle, the rope became even tighter and longer. He also added leaving the scene of an accident, reckless driving, several open bench warrants, and various other motor vehicle infractions. Along with being slammed dunked/arrested, that tight rope had been reduced to threads, causing him to thread his way from that point on.

His girl and the unborn baby turned out fine. And I truly imagine he's still paying his fine.

E.O.S.P.

One midnight tour, the Reverend and I were on patrol in uniform in a marked police vehicle traveling northbound on Clinton Avenue. We were stopped at the traffic light at Astor Street and Clinton Ave. I, the vehicle's operator, looked over at my partner and observed him trying to half heartedly wave off the sleep fairy taking control of his consciousness. So, I decided to start up a conversation to assist his efforts. I said in a loud voice, "Rev, suppose a hold up alarm from the restaurant on our right comes over the police radio right now? What would you do?"

The Rev sleepily and sheepishly said, "Handle it."

I said, "Yeah, we'll be on them like Ali Baba and the Forty Thieves stealing a sleeping beauty princess's sleepwear off her body and not awakening her."

No sooner had the words parted my lips when the dispatcher came over the air waves with, "All south district units respond to restaurant at Clinton Ave. and Astor St. to an armed robbery in progress. No other info at this time." We were right there on the corner, in front of the place at the traffic light. The Rev snapped out of his slowly progressing comatose condition and looked at me as if I was part of the stick up team. I ignored his shocked, disbelieving expression and said, "You ready? Let's go. I call this one E.O.S.P. (extra ordinary sensory perception) at its best." While making a right turn onto Astor St., we notified the dispatcher of our location as we visually surveyed the parking lot and restaurant. Everything was as calm and quiet as a newborn baby smiling in his sleep. We made a right turn into the parking lot, pulling around to the rear and then to the side of the restaurant. We exited our vehicle and approached the rear and front of the restaurant. Everything appeared to be normal. We got the attention of an employee cleaning the dining room who let us in. We surprised the manager and another worker who were in the office because of our quick response. They hadn't expected us so soon. They appeared to be going over what to tell the police. We advised the dispatcher and other responding officers the suspects were G.O.A. (gone on our arrival). We gave out the descriptions that were given to us, flight of the suspects, and prepared the initial police report. Our detective bureau took over the investigation from there. I believed then and today, no actual robbery took place. The manager was covering up for some currency that somehow got into the currents.

I never did find out what really happened. If anyone out there does know, let me in on it. I'll know then if my extraordinary sensory perception needs any adjustments. After resuming our motor patrol duties my partner insisted on knowing how I called that hold-up like I did. I responded with, "I call 'em like I feel 'em," like the number one soul brother of soul and his song "Hah hah I Got The Feeling Hah hah."

POLICE VEHICLE ACCIDENTALLY SHOT

This incident occurred as my partner, the Rev, a.k.a the Preacher, a United States Army Vietnam veteran and a U.S. Air Force Reservist and I (a.k.a. Buck), a happily, but miss-you-all, retired police officer, were working together one evening in uniform and in a marked police vehicle. We were in the area of West Alpine Street and Ridgewood Avenue, when we stopped a just released male ex-convict. He was well chiseled and had a reputation as a tough, small time drug dealer, who didn't take any "s—" from the street tac heads or the man (police). We approached him with probable cause and attempted a frisk for weapons for his and our safety. Since I initiated the frisk, the suspect pushed me away, while spitting verbal salads, "Git the f/friend off me." Luckily, I was able to grab him and hold on until my partner joined in and a full fledged struggle ensued. The fierce struggle began in the street, worked its way up on the sidewalk, back into the street, and then onto the hood of our police vehicle. The superior, stronger suspect began dumping drugs when he wasn't fighting or trying to run. We weren't going to let him get away, but we couldn't wristcuff or contain him. For the first time, as long time partners, we had to request backup assistance as the struggle turned into an all out battle and bordered the lines of life threatening. Even though it was the two of us against him, apparently my partner had enough and believed the battle had well crossed the life threatening line and had become an actual life threatening incident. He pulled his police service weapon (.38) while we were still on top of the police car. In defense of our lives, he fired a desperation shot at the super strong suspect. The shot missed its intended target and went throught the hood of our police vehicle. We discovered later that the shot, fortunately, missed critical engine parts. The sound of the gun shot and/or the bullet passing the suspect, along with his being exhausted, caused him to give up. He laid limp and motionless on top of our vehicle as if he had been shot. We wristcuffed him and checked him for obvious injuries. The back up police officers responded after we had gotten the situation under control. The suspect, now a prisoner, was arrested for an assault on police officers, possession of drugs, and several open bench warrants. However, most of our time was spent submitting reports on the fired shot and subsequent damage to the vehicle.

Until that incident, we were keeping pace with another highly aggressive team known as Batman and Robin, who, as South District Station police officers had never requested back up as partners. Batman was one of the strongest police officers I had ever seen or met. I was working with him once while handling a domestic complaint and observed him, with reason, pick up a three hundred pound plus male by the shirt and jacket. He slid him up a room wall, arms length and caused the man's voice to rise several octaves above his normal voice tone. The problem was quickly remedied. Batman had awesome strength.

My U.S.A. Reserves Partner

On this particular evening my partner, a former U.S.A. Reserves Captain and myself were walking the beat on Bergen Street. On our beat, this one particular drug dealer sold drugs from a porch of an abandoned house on Hunterdon Street and Hawthorne Avenue. He took pride in himself because he didn't have to use a car, confine himself in a building or use runners. He also didn't have to worry about his stash disappearing because he kept his drugs in his pocket and would simply, as he stated, "Outrun the police." He also bragged that the South District Police and Narcotics Squad didn't have the time nor the manpower to send at least five cops to corner him. If they did, he would shake and bake (run) long enough to get rid of his package. So, my partner and I formulated a plan to bring him down. For the plan to work, it had to be raining to limit his mobility and rid the area of the riff raff. On the first hard downpour, after we made our plans, we donned our long black rain coats and black rubber boots then started out on our beat. This dealer would set up by sitting on his porch, where he could see in front, his left and right sides due to the open lots, and he could look to his rear through the busted out windows and doors for "Five o" (police) from the porch. He would only sell to known customers on foot and wave off unknown customers, with an all out or no more signal. If they got too close without his approval, he would simply run off. With this in mind, we left the police station walking east on West Bigelow Street to Jelliff Avenue, through the open lots between Hawthorne Avenue and West Runyon Street. West to Hunterdon Street, where we knew our man would have "shop open." With the rain, we knew he wouldn't have anybody to warn him and wouldn't be walking and checking his surroundings often. We made it up to the abandoned house undetected. I then instructed my partner to slowly walk up from the left side of the house to check and see if he was there. He was, but he peeped (saw) my partner and he leaped from the porch and hit the ground in stride. I could hear that something was on. The suspect was hauling a-- through the lot north on Peshine Avenue. My partner and I got in pursuit. My partner was initially behind him, but with me being the speed merchant of us two, I passed him and got into full galloping stride behind the suspect. As he crossed West Runyon Street, I turned on the after burners (more speed), he continued running toward West Bigelow Street. Now he's continually looking back, knowing that I wasn't about to call it a day. As he crossed West Bigelow Street, the former track star was tiring and was about to be finished before crossing the line. He, on a sneak tip, threw his package (drugs) to the ground on his dog leg (final turn). I made eye contact where the drugs would land and remained locked on the foot pursuit. The suspect finally gave out and dove to the ground from flat out exhaustion. Another one bites the dirt. As he slid across the ground, he threw a piece of rolled up currency into the street, hoping to divert my attention from where the real package landed. I dove on top of the suspect. I used him to crash stop instead of burning the rubber from my boots trying to stop. He was arrested for possession of drugs, wristcuffed, and helped to his feet. After my partner eventually caught up to us and caught his breath, he held onto the prisoner, while I went to retrieve the package he tossed that never left my eyesight. The prisoner began yelling, "Officer, please don't let him put that s— on me, that ain't my s—."

My partner eventually asked him, "What about all that money bulging in your pockets, is that yours?"

The prisoner said, "What money? Oh, this is my girl's s—. I ain't got nothing." I picked up the currency he tossed, unrolled it, and submitted it as additional evidence. He was transported to the police station and processed from that evening on, and for the next few years, I had street level respect for my ability to track a suspect down. The arrested man still lives in the area of the South District today, a one time class sprinter turned a no class street drug merchant.

U.S.M.C. RESERVES PARTNER

The fact that this partner of mine was in the U.S.M.C. is enough said on its own. One night he and I were on patrol west on Chancellor Ave., when we observed a motor vehicle idling with a tail light out. A male driver was behind the wheel, and he was talking to two females at the passenger side front door. As we pulled up behind him in our police van, my partner got out, and the car slowly pulled off. The females began whispering to my partner to stop that car saying the driver had a gun. The vehicle made a u-turn facing east on Chancellor Ave. I made a u-turn to try and stop the vehicle while my partner was still getting information from the females. The vehicle then sped off. My partner came running over to our vehicle, jumped on the rear door step, smacked the side of the van and said, "Go." Oh s— here we go. I sped off east on Chancellor Ave. after the vehicle with my partner hanging off the rear in the air stream. I eventually slowed down after having no chance of catching the car. My partner, after getting back into the van, started spitting verbal salads, "Why did you stop? You ain't got no b———. All you had to do was pull up alongside the damn car and I would've jumped on." I looked at him long and hard trying to figure out what was insane about him.

We returned to the original location to look for the females, but they were gone. So, we eventually went off duty and that was that until the next day. We returned to work the next day and were assigned again to the prisoner transport van.

We went on patrol until we were needed to transport prisoners. While approaching the area of West Runyon St. and Chadwick Ave., we observed a large crowd gathered around an apparent fight going. We parked our van and approached the crowd. To our surprise, there was the car parked that we chased the night before. We then started looking the crowd over while trying to get to the middle. Suddenly, the suspect who had been driving the car and carrying an alleged gun bolted from the crowd. He fled northwest on Chadwick Ave. with us in pursuit. My partner, the speedster of us two, and I, no slouch, was on his tail like a cheap tux with tails. The suspect was quick and agile, but with no wind. He was running so hard, cutting and zigzagging, it appeared he was trying to run into the ground. Each step he took produced chunks of lawn dirt from the lawns as he ran across. He finally fell face first from exhaustion on Chadwick Ave. with both hands under his stomach. My partner, myself, and back up officers had him surrounded as he continued to struggle with the apparent gun in his waistband. As he was running, his gun had slipped down into his briefs, preventing him from discarding it. He probably should've worn boxer shorts that day. After he fell, he actually had gotten hold of the gun's handle, but was too exhausted to pull it out. My partner jumped the fence, removed the gun, wristcuffed him, and he was arrested for the unlawful gun. This was a clear cut case of a young man who was meant to be arrested. We missed him the night before in the short car chase because I had a lot of drag on the rear of the van, but we caught him the next day in the foot chase. My partner is still looking for the prisoner's vehicle that disappeared again after the arrest.

On another particular morning my partner and I were assigned to the prisoner transport van. Again, if you were not transporting prisoners, you went on patrol and handled assignments. We were working the night shift and it was close to quitting time on a very cold morning. So, before we went in, as we always did a little extra, we checked the area of Clinton Ave. and Osborne Ter. That area was a known high crime area then and it still is today. As we approached the area, we came upon an apparent early morning drug deal. One male was eventually apprehended for possession of drugs, and the involved currency was confiscated. Since we interrupted the deal before anything changed hands, the other suspect was released. The charge of wandering wasn't on the books yet. We then placed the prisoner in the van and stood by for the towing of his vehicle. It was freezing cold that morning, so I got in the van, shivering, and tried to warm up. My partner was still on the outside walking around the prisoner's car as if he was still looking for something. All my partner had on was that thin windbreaker police jacket that he always wore without a hat or gloves. I'm sitting in the van colder than a witch's breast in a frozen iceberg. He eventually flipped open the gas tank door on the suspect's car.

I said to myself, "I can see from here there's nothing there. Get in the damn van p (partner) before your b—— freeze, fall off, roll down your pants legs, and get stepped on."

He then unscrewed the gas cap and slowly removed a small caliber handgun from the neck of the gas tank. I damn near jumped through the roof of the van. The prisoner was verbally damning himself damn near through the floor, "Damn, damn." I got out of the van and couldn't congratulate him enough, and I still had a hard time believing, with all the drugs recovered in that cold weather, there was still a gun to be recovered.

My partner ended up being the most determined officer, I

ever trained/broke in, and/or worked with. He had a lot of the U.S.M.C. heart.

This incident occurred on Hawthorne Ave. and Bergen St. in a rooming house, where a 70 year old plus female (a.k.a. Granny) was actively, engaged in a cocaine dispensing business. My partner and I paid her a visit, which was unknown to her until we approached her room. As we were walking in, she was leaving to apparently make a sale with the drugs in her hand. Her customer had fled earlier as we passed him in the hall. After observing us, she turned and flung the several tin foils of cocaine into a plastic bucket, just inside her room door containing battery acid. My partner, who was always concerned about losing evidence, sped over to the bucket and without hesitating, reached in with his bare hand and recovered the cocaine. He then quickly rinsed the cocaine first and then his hand with water from a sink, located in the room. He then handed me the evidence and asked, "I hope you don't have any reservations now about checking them since I did the hard part."

I replied, "Naw, not now, although I wasn't going in that battery acid." The cocaine was still dry and Granny's battery acid toss didn't work resulting in her arrest. Unlawful drug involvement has no prejudices nor limits. It's so low, it has users and others seemingly hang jumping from the curb to get in the gutter and get involved. Granny was still involved in drug activity for some time after that arrest.

On another night, my partner and myself were on patrol, assigned to a marked police vehicle. We were in the area of Clinton Ave. and Hillside Ave., where an abandoned and condemned rooming house was located. The rooming house was being used by drug dealers, drug users, squatters, and others. We had obtained information on this one particular drug dealer, as to what room he was operating out of and the location of his drug stash. We were already made aware that the entrance doors were chained locked from the inside; the rear doors were barricaded and nailed shut; the first floor windows were all barricaded and nailed shut; and the metal fire escapes, aluminum leaders, and gutters had all been removed. There was no way of getting in without making a lot of noise unless we were let in.

We parked our police vehicle a couple of blocks away, walked up to the rooming house and circled it, trying to figure out how to get in. While in the rear yard, my partner suggested I cover the front in case someone left, which would eventually allow us to get in. He continued surveying the rear of the house for any possible point of entry. After a few minutes, no one came out of the front door. I hadn't heard anything from my partner. I quietly walked to the rear of the house to check on his progress if any. My partner had somehow scaled from the ground floor to a third floor window and was climbing in. I don't know how he did it then or now, but he did it. Maybe he had a G.I. Joe Special Operations Kit in his sock. While climbing through the window, he interrupted an elderly couple in bed humping (making passionate love). When I later asked him who was on top, he wouldn't say. He did say as he was walking past the two nude involved people, he excused and identified himself as he let himself out of their room. The lovers didn't bother to stop and relock their door. He walked down the stairs, quietly unchained the door and let me in.

We rechained the door in case the suspect got passed us, making it difficult for him to escape. We quietly walked back up the stairs to the third floor, found and knocked on the target room door. A suspect known as TMGH (Too Much Git High) opened the door. He had a peep hole on his door, but didn't bother to use it because he probably thought we were regulars. After Too Much Git High opened his room door, we invited ourselves in while he was in the process of trying to be rude and shut the door in our faces. We frisked him with negative results and told him to sit down, shut up, and listen to us. We then explained to him, he was there unlawfully and we had information he was selling 24/7. Too Much Git High nervously said, "Damn man, I'm carrying a stick (carrying a stick means all of your earthy belongings tied up in a piece of cloth tied to the end of a stick), like everybody else in this m'f (my friend)." As he made that statement, he broke (ran) for the door. He was vigorously warned not to try that again as he slowly got up from the floor. My partner with his speed was the first one to reach him. After Too Much Git High got himself together he said, "Word is bond. I won't try that again." Shortly after that, his stash, cocaine and heroin, was removed from the garbage can. He was eventually advised and arrested for unlawful possession of the drugs, trespassing, and several open bench warrants. As we were leaving, we made several loud announcements that everybody there was trespassing, had to leave and that we would be back. As we unchained the door to leave, Too Much Git High insisted on knowing how we got in. We informed him that if he found that out, we couldn't come back the same way. The building was eventually torn down before we kept our "We'll be back" promise, I believe that arrest and the ensuing complaints concerning our entry techniques sped up the demolition process.

LET'S TAKE A STAND WITH GOD

Let's reach out and hold a hand
And help someone in need of a helping hand
Let's help each other become part of God's plans
And disregard our own selfish plans
Let's take a stand
And make it stand

Let's pray for each other
And it doesn't matter, we may not know one another
Let's get it together and stay together
And make it easy for God to keep us together

Let's fast and pray today
And ask God to forgive and help whoever is gay
Let's ask God to erase the craving for nicotine in sickarettes
    and as in cigarettes
Let's ask God to erase the habit forming craving for sickars
    and as in cigars
Let's ask God to turn drug doers around
In their tracks
And become doers of God's words and
Tracts

Let's ask God to help the evening ladies on the stroll
And help them get their God given bodies under his control
Let us pray and ask God to change the crime learning prisons
And help the inmates become God fearing daughters and
    sons
Let's fast and pray
And ask our dear God to help us to always fast and pray

Excuse Me Please, For One Moment

_____Then you can return to this book_____

What do you call **A** person who forcibly **T**akes

things from other people and **H**angs around on

street corners like a neck tie instead of being like a hat

and going on a head of someone with ambition, is

Ungodly and **G**rossly misinformed about everything,

from washing their **ass to** being part of the **z**oo crew?

If you didn't figure out the above answer, try answering the next question:

What do you call **A** person who's holding down a street corner with long baggy pants on dragging **T**hrough dog and cat "hit," also any other animal or human waste that may be on t**H**e gro**U**nd, with each drag of the bottom of his pant's legs. He's pacing back and forth making eye contact with every passing motorist (checking for possible customers, one time-five o or the "f'in**G**/friendly" police and/or his hit'em up rivals) and has his underwear (partially) covered gay buttocks exposed. There's no one else around mostly out of fear and he's rapidly moving his lips (as in talkin**G**). You don't know **I**f he's talking to him**S**elf, t**H**e devil (which is the opposite of lived, he did live and walked on earth as we do now at one time) rapping, talking to his p/partner/s that was recently hit up (killed)/with an express one way ticket to hell or on a hands free cellular telephone. You may not want to know what's going on or off, other **T**han **H**is event**U**ally **G**oing off the deep end of hell to join his p (who he had mad love for) with no r.i.p.e./rest in peace ever. Prior to

45

going off the deep you find out he's disrespectful to God and all that He stands for. He walks around in front of his mother and sisters with his exposed, underwear-covered, gay butt sticking out, his belt tightly securing the waistband of his pants around his knees. He exhales third and fourth hand drug induced blunt smoke, along with spouting profanity at will throughout his mother's crowded home. He's a high school kick out, can't or won't hold down a lawful job, has trouble maintaining his unlawful street merchant status and he has your sixteen-year-young daughter's home telephone/cellular/beeper-pager numbers and school/home addresses in his watch pocket.

Reread the above sentencess for clues if you didn't find the answer/s, and by the way, do you know where your son, brother, man, friend, associate, significant other or husband is?

CHAPTER III

THE ELUSIVE FISH BOWLS

My partner, known as Wild Bill, passed the sergeant's examination and would've have been on his way up the success ladder if he hadn't retired. As he was retiring, he was working very hard toward becoming a movie director or someone along those lines. He was a very good and active partner, very brilliant, witty and loved to write. He also had or still has a very beautiful wife.

This incident occurred as Wild Bill and I were on patrol, in uniform and in a marked police vehicle. While traveling north on Badger Avenue between Madison Avenue and Avon Avenue in an area known as the Fish Bowl, we observed an idling vehicle facing northbound occupied by three males, two seated in the front and one seated in the rear. They appeared not to see us, initially, as we pulled up alongside their vehicle because all three were preoccupied with hitting/snorting from bags of suspected dope/heroin. I hit/sounded my vehicle horn to get their attention. They looked at us wide eyed and with wide opened dope mouths. Wild Bill motioned with his fingers for the operator to shut the vehicle's ignition off. The vehicle's operator, instead dropped the gear selector in low and accelerated off north on Badger Ave., then east on Avon Ave. and south on Irvine Turner Boulevard with us right behind them with our emergency lights and siren on, trying to get the driver to stop. The police dispatcher was notified. The pursuit crossed Clinton Ave., West Alpine Street, W. Bigelow St., W. Runyon St. and proceeded onto Highway 78. As the suspect's late model, brand new looking vehicle increased speed, we decreased our vehicle's speed, being particularly aware of an oncoming tight turn. We slowed to almost a crawl, knowing that imminent disaster lay ahead, especially at their reckless speed. As we slowly proceeded onto the highway and came out of that tight turn, the suspect's vehicle was now facing us. It had spun around and slammed to a stand still up against a concrete wall. Apparently while the suspect's vehicle was turning on two wheels, the driver applied the new brakes. The one brake applied wheel with the momentum of the turn caused their vehicle to slam into the wall in a tight one hundred eighty degree circle, totaling out the right side of their vehicle.

As we pulled up in front of the suspect's vehicle, the occupants appeared to be dead or unconscious. We activated our adrenalin induced siren and all three suspects, appeared to snap out of their unconscious or drug induced states, with that "Oh s—" look on their faces. They then, frantically, tried to get out of the left side of their vehicle. We exited our vehicle and were on them like a "low cut, short tight dress, with splits on a perfect size 10." They were expeditiously extracted from their vehicle.

The driver was subsequently arrested for eluding officers and for open bench warrants. His two passengers for open bench warrants after they, believe it or not, indicated they were not injured. The drugs had vanished, either in the air stream or down their throats. The totaled out vehicle was towed. It belonged to the unlicensed driver's girlfriend. Believe this: he's on drugs, unemployed, unkempt, unmanly, unreal, unschooled, unwise and whole lot of other un's. His girlfriend unbelievably allowed him to use her vehicle, in which he almost put three people to sleep permanently. The Fish Bowl can turn up some slippery and wild catches. This turnedout to be three of them.

FISH BOWL TALE II

Another incident occurred on the same above street, Badger Ave., in The Fish Bowl. I was working in uniform as a one police officer unit in the huge marked neighborhood stabilization unit (NSU) van on the evening shift (1600-0000 hours). I happened upon an idling, white, marked United States postal van that stood out in that area like Santa Claus in June on the broadwalk in Atlantic City clad in only his boots and hat. Upon investigating, I found an older male, the van's operator, in the rear of the van with a lady of the evening. Both were quickly adjusting their clothing. A condom was in plain view on the floor of the van. I didn't check to see if it was used or unused. I asked the extremely nervous and trembling operator for his driving credentials.

He complied and stated, "Officer I'm a postal supervisor, and my job is on the line if this gets out, and I'm due to retire soon."

I responded with, "Okay, let me confer with my supervisor." I requested a supervisor from the police dispatcher. A field sergeant responded and basically said if I or anyone else didn't observe any criminal activity, field interview both of them and thoroughly check the driver's driving credentials, and be guided by the those results. They were both record checked, with no holds, sent on their way in different directions and before leaving, the postal supervisor couldn't thank me enough. He actually should've been thanking God and not me. It was God who spared him from possible AIDS, from being robbed, arrested or even killed. The Fish Bowl lured them from all professions and some of them left a little fishy.

Fish Bowl Tale III

Another incident of the many in The Fish Bowl occurred as my partner, Wild Bill, and I were working together in a marked police vehicle in uniform on the evening shift (1600-0000). It was dark out and toward the end of our shift when we decided to give the Fish Bowl one more tactical passing. While traveling north on Badger Ave., a criminally active, desolate area between Madison and Avon Avenues, we came upon an idling vehicle, occupied by the operator and a front seat passenger.

I was driving our police vehicle and Wild Bill was the observer as we pulled up alongside the idling vehicle unnoticed by the occupants. The two occupants were deeply preoccupied in what had all the appearances of drug activity. The female operator of the idling vehicle was looking intensely down toward her lap and her passenger was intensely eyeballing whatever she was doing with her hands. I hit/turned on our vehicle's overhead right alley light, which lit up the front inside of their vehicle. The female operator was a police officer and she looked up, shocked, and looked directly in Wild Bill's face in an apparent continued state of shock.

I said, "Let's check them."

Wild Bill said, "No, pull off."

I said, "I'm checking them," and I started to get out of our vehicle.

Wild Bill, while growing furious, said, "No, no, let's go." So I let my door handle go and pulled off. The female officer only saw Wild Bill, neither her or her passenger saw me. I recognized her, but I didn't see her passenger's face too clearly. That officer, after that chance meeting, stopped speaking to Wild Bill from that time on, up to the point of his retirement. She continued to speak to me in passing. Some people get caught out there like that when they pull over in the Fish Bowl where the fishing was easy at that time.

FISH BOWL TALE IV

This peculiar and unusual incident occurred on a midnight tour, very early in my long police career in an area, years later, to be known as The Fish Bowl. We observed a male limping southbound on a street known then as Belmont Avenue, now known as Irvine Turner Boulevard, named in honor of a politician. My partner and I were in a marked police vehicle, traveling in the same direction on that quiet and warm early morning. My partner, the driver, pulled up alongside the limping man, and I asked him if everything was all right. While asking him that question, I observed a suspicious looking bulge on his right side. The tall male looked down at us, recognized my observation of the bulge, and I guess he figured, enough is enough. He broke/ran from our conversation, south on Belmont Ave., then west on Clinton Avenue. After exiting our vehicle, I ran after him and was quickly on his heels. He was running and at times skipping, as if he had something very long stuck down his right pant's leg. He then ran and skipped northbound into a debris strewn lot. My partner drove the police vehicle to Madison Avenue and Badger Avenue to await the suspect and cut off his possible escape route. Once the suspect got into the lot, his skipping, limping, and stumbling got the best of him causing him to tumble to the ground. I initially kept my tactical distance behind him, not sure if the bulging object that went from his waist down to his ankle was a rifle, shotgun, or some other weapon. I had him like a fast hungry lion stalking a slow and limping jackal all the way and wasn't worried about him getting away. After he fell down in the lot, I could clearly see the butt end of what turned out to be a rifle protruding from his waistband and down his stretched out right leg. I ordered him at gun point to remain on the ground and not move until my partner arrived. After the rifle was pulled out of his pant's leg, he was arrested for the unlawful possession of a firearm and wristcuffed.

A very important point for all police officers to remember

concerning law breakers is they need to stay on the lam. This particular suspect ran almost a block and a half with a rifle stuck down his pant's leg. I've had several suspects and prisoners run while wristcuffed from behind. Most of them got caught, but they'll still run and try you. Another very important point to remember is that a prisoner is never in secured custody until he hears that sound "SLAM" from his cell door slamming closed and locked, which is how the word "SLAMMER" originated.

Prisoners and suspects are more prone to attempt an escape today than ever before, cuffed or uncuffed, because they can't seem to take jail. They also seem to think police officers can't, won't, or don't like to run. I ran after all of them.

While we're on the subject of cuffs, I don't know where the term "Handcuffs," came from, when it's your wrists that are cuffed, which is why I'm using the term wristcuffs all through this novel. Ankle braces are sometimes referred to as leg braces, when they're actually bracing the ankles. Neck braces, popular during slavery times, were not called head or body braces, but neck braces because they went around the neck. Remember a lot of deadly things can still be accomplished with cuffed hands.

THE FISH BOWL TALE V

On this evening, I was assigned to a one officer patrol unit, and during the course of my patrol duties, I happened upon the Fish Bowl area to go "fishing." I came upon a motor vehicle parked, but idling, with a delinquent motor vehicle inspection sticker. A male operator was behind the wheel. I eventually u-turned, pulled in behind him, called in his plate number, and got out to check his driving credentials. He didn't have any and it wasn't his car, so I asked him to have a seat in my vehicle for the issuance of at least summonses and a record check. While I was waiting on the plate check to come in over the radio, I walked over to the vehicle and began checking the glove compartment for the registration and insurance card. While I was involved with looking for the vehicle's paper work, I heard an automobile horn sounding. Aware of no other vehicles being in the area, I looked back at my vehicle and to my shocking surprise, the suspect was climbing from the rear seat to the front of my vehicle through the little window on the metal partition which separates rear seat occupants from the officers in the front seat. As he was climbing through he had to grab the steering wheel, to pull his long body through the window, which is how he inadvertently hit my vehicle's horn. The suspect was at least 6' 2" tall and weighed 190 lbs. I ran to the driver's side of my vehicle to prevent him from getting behind the wheel and pulling off. After pulling himself through the window, he then fled out of the passenger/observer right front side of my vehicle and hit the ground running.

This incident happened late in my police department career, but I still had enough regular gas in my tank to run him down during the foot chase. Naturally, the vehicle came back stolen. After I caught him he was wristcuffed, advised of his rights, and brought back to my vehicle, charged accordingly and issued several much deserved summonses. I was spared the embarrassment because no one found out what had happened—until now.

Remember officers: Keep that little window on your partition closed at all times. If the suspect hadn't hit my vehicle's horn, he would've gotten into the driver's seat, then quietly drove off in my marked police vehicle and left me quietly stranded in the Fish Bowl swimming in my own perspiration. Some prisoners and/or suspects will try any means necessary to escape at your expense, so pay attention now, so you'll continue to get paid your pay check later.

THE FISH BOWL VI

The area of Hunterdon Street and Madison Avenue was a desolate area at the time. Most of the houses and businesses had been torn down. The area had become a place where a lot of people chose to come and conduct criminal activity. It was an area was from Hunterdon Street east to Irvine Turner Blvd. and Clinton Avenue north to Avon Avenue. It was so named the Fish Bowl by a partner of mine, Wild Bill, and I added, "where the fishing for criminals was easy."

On this particular occasion I was assigned to a marked police vehicle in uniform with a female officer. I was driving and she was the observer. I spotted an idling vehicle with a male behind the wheel, and he appeared from a distance to be involved in some type of suspicious activity. As we pulled up and partially blocked his vehicle from a possible escape route, he appeared to be snorting drugs with one hand and doing something with the other hand. Once out of our vehicle we could see he was trying to remove something large and long from the inside rear of his pants, we drew our guns and ordered him out of his vehicle thinking he had a weapon. What he eventually pulled out of the rear of his pants, to our bewilderment was a six to eight inch black, fat dildo, which definitely could've been a weapon). He had been hitting himself in the butt while snorting dope in his vehicle parked on a city street during the early evening.

We towed his vehicle, issued summonses, and arrested him for the unlawful possession of heroin. My partner and I were totally shocked out of our minds. She couldn't believe what she had just seen. I don't know if she ever repeated what we observed that day, I know she'll never forget it.

The suspect eventually stated he was having problems but didn't elaborate. He refused our request to get him medical attention we offered because I thought he might have injured himself since he was a thin person and the dildo was very long, but apparently he was quite use to what he was doing. He probably has a family at his home, unaware of his side street Fish Bowl activities. We, as aggressive and concerned police officers, have to deal with such occurrences and then some. We then hopefully return home to our beloved families and try to interrelate with them with a normal frame of mind. May God please guide all of us, in all that we do, see and fish out of the Fish Bowl.

THE FISH BOWL VII

This was a police action involving my partner, known as Fitz, and myself on Irvine Turner Boulevard between Madison Avenue and Avon Avenue. We observed a male involved in drug activity. We stopped our vehicle to investigate and apprehend if necessary. The male suspect fled into an apartment building up to the third floor with us in hot foot pursuit, dropping drugs as he was fleeing. The male suspect eventually fled into an apartment and before the door could be locked behind him, we ran in. The suspect then ran into a closet where he was eventually apprehended, arrested for cocaine, crack form, and for possession of weapons, four revolvers. The weapons were in the closet as a result of his obtaining them from customers for drugs in lieu of money, and he probably forgot the guns were in the same closet he ran into.

I've confronted drug dealers that will sell their drugs for money, jewelry, weapons, other drugs, food stamps, vehicles, sex and whatever else you have to exchange. Fitz was an excellent partner. He was an exceptional song and dance man. He was also well liked by most of the ladies he confronted. Fitz left the department for personal reasons prior to my retirement.

LORD GUIDE US

Dear Lord draw us near
To you to hide a tear
We always seem to shed as we fear
The things we hear
That can be heard by any willing ear
As our hearts worry and wear
We know you'll be there to bear
And continue to be dear
In our hearts as you Dear Lord draw us near.

FAST AND PRAY

Fast and pray to
Cast away any doubt that our Lord's Love will
Last forever and forever,
Let not a moment be in the past
And you haven't uttered, "I thank and love you Lord,"
Be as a strong mast on a ship
And steady yourself in troubled waters, be as
A strong bast that firms the rope, that hoists the anchor, that
    controls
A ship at rest and
Cast away all your doubts, hoist your achor and set your
Sails toward heaven.

Readdress your interest in this novel or be prepared to read
the following:

DRESS THAT DEPRESS

Yo flip that wrong side wearing shirt
On the right side

Fore u get flipped
On your left side

Get that shirt flipped
And hurry right back
Fore u get left back
Cause u ain't no middle back, full back, tail back, flanker
    back, ½ back or ¼ back
My back, yo you ain't ? u know what, u know what

Flip those wrong side wearing pants
Flip that tee shirt off your head
Looking like a witch on a head hunt
With no brew, with no brew, with no brew
Looking like dew, dew, dew, dew

Get your act together
From head to toe before u react
Slip up, down and altogether

In your own u know what, u know what
Flip that wrong side wearing shirt
Fore u get hit from the blind as- side
Flip those wrong side wearing pant's pockets
Looking like you're on the broke as- side

Flip that head wearing tee shirt,
Playing it like head wear.
Stop wearing underwear as outer wear,
Stop wearing inside nite wear as outside outer wear.

Take that sales tag
Off your dress wear and foot wear.
Looking like a fag as-playing tag ,
Fore you get bagged and for real tagged,
With your ragged looking as-.

Tie those strings up on your footwear,
Fore u get tripped up
And get ripped and dipped down
In u know what, in u know what.

Stop dressing to depress,
Stop dressing to depress,
With yo unpressed dressed as-,
With yo unpressed dressed as-.

CHAPTER IV

SOME OF MY MOST
UNUSUAL ARRESTS

This incident is one of those unusual seventies (1971) incidents. I was working with an officer known as Joe and his name is still known as simply Joe. I, at the time, was still a green rookie, considered by fellow police officers to be too skinny. I looked and walked too slow even though I could pick'em up and put'em down (run) with the best of them. I was also considered to be too thin at six feet, one and half inches tall and one hundred forty five pounds light to win at anything. I was thought to have very little hand skills, if any, and if I got into a long argument, I would probably pass out from exhaustion. Nevertheless, we were in uniform, assigned to a marked police vehicle and 511 sector, which is from Osborne Terrace to Fabyan Place east to west and Nye Avenue to Field Place north to south. While in our sector and seated in our police vehicle at a stop light near Chancellor Avenue and Aldine Street, an over excited male citizen ran up to the driver's side of our police vehicle where I was seated and said, "Officer, there's something strange going on in that bar on the corner." He pointed wildly toward Aldine St. and Chancellor Ave. The male citizen then, excitedly and hurriedly, ran off.

My partner said, "Pull over there near the lounge and let's check it out." I pulled over southbound on Aldine St. We got out of our vehicle, my partner with all of the above adjectives concerning me, fresh on his mind, sent me to the front door of the lounge on the Chancellor Ave. side, and he went to the rear door on the Aldine St. side. While slowly walking toward the front door and notifying the police dispatcher of our intentions, my speedy partner dashed past me. After he had already checked the rear door window, apparently observing something, he then looked in the front door window, again observing something. He, with that "Oh s—" look on his face, dashed from the front door back to the rear door without saying a word to me as to what was going on in the lounge. Now I'm thinking, it might be a fight or some type of brawl going on. As my partner got back to the rear door, whoever was doing what on the inside was now running out the rear door. My partner looked back at me with that "I messed up" look and yelled, "You stay here and get some back up," and he started chasing the suspects. During the foot chase, the suspects started shooting at him and he returned fire. Several shots were exchanged. I was on the portable radio, frantically requesting back up.

The back up officers arrived in bunches in a matter of moments and flooded the area. Due to their quick response, a back up officer located one suspect hiding under a nearby porch, still armed with a loaded gun. He was taken into custody without incident and arrested. With his cooperation, his come-along buddies in crime were later arrested.

When my partner told me, a still wet-behind-the-ears rookie, to stay at the lounge while he chased the suspects who turned out to be armed, I still don't know if he was worried about my safety, if he thought other suspects were in the lounge or if it was because he, being an ex-track star, was much faster. Also, I never figured out why he didn't remain at the rear door.

With me at the front door, the suspects would've been trapped inside. Whatever the reason and taking all the lines, top, middle, bottom, and in between, into consideration, I'm still alive, and he's still alive, and no one was injured, and all of the suspects were eventually caught. So, in between my partner's speedy fifty yard dashes between the front and rear doors, it turned out to be the correct track course of action to the finish line. That was my first and only at-the-scene, armed robbery in progress during my police career.

My partner submitted all of the police reports, and he went to court. I don't know if he received any type of police departmental award for that assignment p.a./police action. He deserved one, especially since he was shot at. I didn't get an award, not that I was looking for one. All I got were a lot of stares and glares from other patrolmen.

Hip Pocket Info For All Police Officers

Always communicate with your partner/s and keep each other informed as much as possible. The above was one of the ways many things happened back in the happening seventies. Biscuit toed, split toed, wing tipped shoes; high collared double breasted suits; short sleeved, buttoned down men's sweaters; pinned/shadow stripped suits; Banlon shirts; and the saying, "All that's good was also there," and Joe is still simply known as just Joe. Richard is still just simply known as not **Rich,** but **hard** and fair. Remember all uniformed officers wink at all little kids when you see them with their parents whenever you get a chance. It's a way of saying hello without making a sound. You'll also be surprised at the number of little kids that can't wink with both eyes, one at a time.

This particular incident, I had the pleasure of working with a police lieutenant. We were in The South District Police Station on an arrest, and I walked out to get a completed police report from our police vehicle. While outside, a speeding motor vehicle traveling east on West Bigelow Street screeched up to the curb, almost hitting me. I jumped out of the way, thinking it was someone with an emergency. A young adult male, a wannabe gangsta type, from the neighborhood popped out of the vehicle and said, "Allen, this car is stolen, lock me the f/ friend up."

I said, "Okay, let's go in and talk to the Desk Lieutenant. I informed him what had transpired outside. He said, "Let him have a seat, check out the registration and VIN (vehicle identification number) on the vehicle."

The vehicle check came back as a reported stolen vehicle and the lieutenant was advised. He said, "Okay, lock him up." The young male, now a prisoner, was taken into the prisoner's detention room and advised of his charge. He was searched and a sizeable amount of cocaine was found and removed from his pant's pockets. The unemotional, on-something prisoner was then charged with unlawful possession of cocaine, which left all of us completely puzzled and looking at each other. He was placed on the bench and one wrist was cuffed to that bench. After cuffing him, I turned my back and began walking away from the prisoner. The prisoner took that opportunity to leap from the bench and with one hand, grabbed my .38 caliber, *Smith and Wesson* handgun and attempted to rip it from my holster. The force of his grip tore my holster. The Desk Lieutenant was watching everything with a bird's eye view from his desk. He eventually suffered, chest pains and had to be taken to the hospital.

In the meantime, my partner and other officers ran to my aid. My partner hit the prisoner with one of the hardest punches I have ever seen thrown. I was frantically holding my gun down into my holster with both hands. My partner's punch and other punches caused the prisoner's hand to become dislodged from my gun. I don't know if my partner's punch or my gun being pulled out of my holster caused the lieutenant's possible heart attack, or if it was the culmination of events. He was medically cleared at the hospital and was eventually released. After order was restored, the tough prisoner, now a certified lumped up gangster, refused medical attention and was hit with several other charges. The same nonpareil prisoner was shot and killed on a hit order not far from the police station where he staged The Most Peculiar Arrest Ever. He may have been killed for not accomplishing his earlier task in the police station. His last dying words, while lying in the street waiting for an ambulance, with bullet holes burned all through his body, "I'm going out like a trooper. I'm going out like a trooper." He then closed his eyes for the very last time. He lost his life, and I earlier, lost a few dollars on a new holster.

We never uncovered the prisoner's actual motive for wanting to be arrested and then making a last ditch attempt to grab my gun. It was buried with him. I always believed that someone in that area knew what was up or down concerning that incident but it's still a mystery.

I don't think the good lieutenant worked the desk again, especially if I was working. Always remember to watch your back and each other's backs and be leary of peculiar acting prisoners. Good looking out to my partner and fellow officers. I still owe all of you one or more.

My "A" Award Incident
Drug Related Armed Robbery/Shooting

My partner Fitz and I were on patrol one evening, in the area of Lyons Avenue and Wainwright Street. While traveling west on Lyons Avenue, a crowd of people started running in the street and on the sidewalk toward us, shouting and screaming, "They're shooting back there," pointing back westward toward Lyons Avenue and Wainwright Street. The crowd was so thick, my partner couldn't move the police car nor could we see past them. I exited our vehicle and started running west on Lyons Avenue to expedite getting past the crowd. Once I got through the crowd, I observed two males on the corner of Lyons Avenue and Wainwright Street, jumping around like they were playing hop scotch. One was armed with what looked like an uzi (machine gun) and the other one was armed with a handgun. After they both appeared to observe me, they began running north on Wainwright Street and then westward through a yard toward Schley Street. By that time, my partner made it through the crowd with the police vehicle, and I signaled him to continue on west toward Schley Street. As I continued to chase both suspects on foot through the yard, the suspect with the uzi fired a shot toward me. I returned fire. They both continued running. The suspect who had the handgun, a point three eighty, loaded, automatic, dropped it on the sidewalk, prior to running into the yard. The suspect who had the uzi dropped it in the yard after I returned fire and barely missed him. A bullet hole burned in the right side of his shirt, which we later recovered, provided verification. My partner eventually apprehended the suspect armed with the handgun on Schley Street. The other suspect was later arrested at his home by detectives in the Dayton Street area.

We eventually learned, after recovering both guns, that the suspects had shot another black male in the groin in an apparent street, drug related robbery. We later arrested the shooting victim at the hospital for the drugs he still had in his possession. The two suspects, the shooters, were charged with gun possession, robbery, assault on a police officer, and various other charges. The suspect's uzi jammed (stove piped). A round had turned upside down in the discharge port, preventing it from firing again, which explains why he was only able to fire once. Both suspects pled guilty in court and served time. The suspect who had the uzi is presently in jail on a homicide charge. The only sad thing about this assignment is that, my partner only got a "C" award, while I received an "A" award. I never told him about my award, but he'll know now.

Lot Fire

Police officer J.D. and myself were assigned together as uniform partners in a marked police vehicle. While on patrol, we came across two obvious drug suspects in a lot on the corner of Astor Street and Frelinghuysen Avenue on their hand and knees looking for something in the dark using cigarette lighters. They explained to us that they had lost a gold chain while funning and were trying to find it. We took their explanation to heart, but also explained they might start a fire in the dark, and we couldn't let them use our flashlights to look for a "b— s—" chain, and they would have to return in the morning to continue their search. They took exception to the "b— s—" part, but they unwillingly agreed and left.

J.D. and I continued on with our patrol duty responsibilities. We stayed in the immediate area in case they returned. While in the area, we ran into and had to politely ask several ladies of the evening on the stroll to move on. Some of them claimed they were walking in the streets because they were afraid to walk on the sidewalks due to the high crime rate in the area, and it was too hot to wear under garments. Others claimed they were giving directions to out of town, misdirected male and bisexual female motorists that just happened to be slowly driving through that high crime area. They had their high beam lights beamed on the ladies no underwear, low cut blouses, and short skirts.

During my many years of police duty, I've seen some of the evening ladies completely nude and others nude from the waist up. Before the always-on-the-job ladies of the evening were finished with their list of excuses, a call came over the air waves with reference to firemen being shot at while fighting a bush fire in a lot at Astor St. and Frelinghuysen Ave. We had to abort our very tough task at hand and eyes of moving the ladies on and volunteer to handle the fire fighters request for police assistance by responding. Since we were just there prior to the call, we figured our same suspects might be involved. We planned our approach to the scene by pulling halfway up Frelinghuysen Ave. between Astor St. and Emmet Street. We exited our vehicle and walked to the now wet lot, where the two previously encountered suspects were again on their hands and knees with cigarette lighters looking. We sneaked up on them and had to physically detain them until the fire chief arrived and identified them as two of the three suspects who interfered with fighting the bush fire. The fire chief further informed us that they had received a call in reference to a fire in a lot. They responded from across the street where the fire house is located on Astor St. and Sherman Avenue with one engine truck and began extinguishing the fire. The two suspects now in custody began yelling, "Get the f/friendly out of here. Y'all wetting our s— up." The fire fighters not knowing what they were talking about, ignored them, and continued fighting the fire. A third suspect stepped out of the darkness, pulled out a firearm, and said, "Hey, fire ladies, y'all got enough wet stuff to put out this fire?" He started busting off/shooting. The City of Newark's bravest dropped their hoses jumped in their fire truck and sped out of the lot, almost jackknifing the truck with the hoses dragging behind. Luckily, none of the fire fighters were injured. Neither the fire truck nor the fire house was damaged as they hurriedly sped in. The suspect with the gun left prior to our arrival. The two suspects under arrest were later found to have been working for the shooter. The shooter had ordered them to return to the lot to look for the contents of a package, his drugs, they tossed while running from earlier stick up men. J.D. and I again politely went out of our way and did the suspects an unthankful favor. We found some or most of their lost package and charged them accordingly. One of the suspects had to be sutured at University Hospital and released for injuries resulting from resisting our efforts to lawfully arrest him as the charges mounted. That old cliché "if you play with fire, you may get burned," should also include, "if you play with fire, you may get locked up and/or if you play with fire fighters fighting a fire, you may get burned and locked up." As I retired J.D. was still a proud member of the City of Newark N.J.'s finest, and the above fire house is still standing, where some of the City of Newark N.J.'s bravest are still making their stand.

DEAR LORD, I TRULY THANK YOU FOR BEING WHO YOU ARE

I truly thank you, Dear Lord, for the love and care
You have truly shown throughout time, which isn't rare
As you have repeatedly shown your love, and I dare
Anyone with anything to the contrary to bare
It, here and now. There's nothing to compare
To our Lord God's shown love, nothing can fare
Nor equal the love that Our Lord is made of. Always beware
Of the false witnesses, they're a day and a nightmare
Lying in wait, in a field of tar
As a hiding hare
Trying to scare
No one but themselves, as we are in,
Our Dear Lord God's care.

Hold up for a minute and let's clear the air—

FOR THE LOVE OF UNLAWFUL HEROIN

Yo, unlawful heroin can make u look as low, as slow moving
slugs
And looking like ur dragging a pair of dried up jugs.

Yo, u with that white creamy sticky stuff in the corners of
your dope mouth mugs
And walking as if ur pockets, shoes and shoulder bags are
filled with lugs.

Yo, ur clothing looks like a bunch of maggots, that defecated
on their after birth rugs
And what's left of ur friends, they're too much afraid of ur
tugs and hugs

Yo, ur only company is the stench craving lice, fleas, ticks
and other flesh eating bugs

And u should check ur selves.
Yo, before u end up deep sixing ur selves

And hanging with ur heads bobbing up and down like u
wanna suck wood
Yo, being for real, we know yours is already dead wood

COCAINE

Yo, u unlawful users may as well crash your head through a
window pane
Or lie n the road and get run over by a great dane

Yo, ur doing unlawful cocaine, n crack form, aka ready
rock n the fast lane
Which is displeasing to **God** and far from being sane

Yo, there's nothing about cocaine, which is reason enough
to use it, then conceive and bear deformed children, it's
insane.

Yo, ur causing your family, society and your self too much
pain
With nothing ever insight to gain
When u cry, it's like chemical rain
When you pretend you want **help**, it's all n vain

Turn to **Our** Almighty God and disdain
From the very less almighty cocaine

MARIJUANA/MARIHUANA

Marijuana is indeed and name, a very foreign and
uncontrolled dangerous substance

Once it enters your God given body, it does a foreign brain
dance

It affects ur stance,
Maybe u don't wanna be too right nor upright.

It puts u in like a trance,
Maybe u don't want to look right nor act right.

It can put u on the wrong side of a lance,
Maybe u don't wanna be on the side of right.

It causes u to take on an unnecessary chance,
Maybe u don't like things all right.

Do the right thing
And give marijuana the left (I left it alone) thing.
So you can be right back in your God given drug free life
And not be left back in satan's hell of a life.

CHAPTER V

OFF DUTY MAN'S ARRESTS

On one evening in 1971 as a pure rookie cop, I was walking home from The Newark Police 5th Precinct in street clothes. I didn't even own a private car yet. While walking in the area of Sherman Avenue and Emmet Street, an older male called out to me from a rooming house window and asked me if I wanted to do something. I guess I looked the part, walking slow and looking tired, which is my regular look. I stopped, looked up, and asked, "Do what?"

He said, "Get high."

I said, "On what?"

He threw me the key and said, "Come on up and see."

I unlocked the door and went to his room, where he met me at the door and ushered me in. I said, "What you got?"

He replied, "Stuff," and showed me several glassine packets of heroin. He then asked me, "How much you need?"

I said, "Damn, bro, I didn't bring any scratch (money) with me."

He said, "They call me Root Man. Can you get some gold (money)?"

I said, "Yeah, but I have to come back."

He said, "Bet, just hurry back."

I said, "Solid (meaning "okay, it's a deal"). Be right back."

I left the rooming house, happy and in a hurry, allowing him to think I was anxious to make the buy. I went to a nearby telephone booth, called the incident into police headquarters and requested a narcotics unit. The dispatcher said, "It's the weekend. Narcotics is off," which was normal at that time.

I said, "Send a tactical/tac unit." At that time, they worked in unmarked cars, but in uniform. I waited, but the tactical unit never arrived, I called back and requested a marked police unit. I waited again but they never arrived. I guess by being a rookie I didn't have that authoritarian or familiar voice. Remember that rookies. I didn't get any help, so I began thinking I couldn't let Root Man get away. I have to do this myself, even without wristcuffs, being a rookie. I went back to the rooming house and rang the superintendent's bell. He happened to be an auxiliary police officer with wrist cuffs. I identified myself and explained the situation to him. We formalized a simple plan. We then went upstairs. I knocked on Root man's door. He opened the door, smiled, and said, "You got the gold?"

I said, "Yeah, you got the s— (the dope)?"

He said, "Yeah, how many you want?"

The auxiliary officer was still outside the door out of sight, when he observed me initiate the bum rush. He joined in, and we wristcuffed Root Man. I informed him he was under arrest for what turned out to be twenty-five packets of heroin, a street value of about five hundred dollars, which was a nice size quantity at the time. The auxiliary officer fled back to his room to call backup on his room phone. Several police officers arrived on the scene, looking puzzled after having heard the earlier request for a tactical and marked unit. It took me several hours to finish all of the reports on my very first off duty arrest and first arrest without a partner. Root Man eventually pled guilty in court and I never saw him or heard anything about him after that incident.

He apparently was a small time drug dealer and a big time user in the seventies.

Remember rookies—always be prepared on and off duty for the unexpected. Also, you may or may not get the expected back up exactly when you need it.

RELENTLESS

This one morning I had just gotten off work from my part time security job at a popular restaurant on Elizabeth Avenue. I then went to another popular restaurant on Frelinghuysen Avenue to eat breakfast. Just as I sat down with my tray to eat, a security guard came in the back door, looked at me, and asked if I was a police officer. I looked down at my police shirt, police patches, badge, and gun belt, then back up at him and said, "Yes."

He stated, "I have a problem. I work for the airport and this guy stole two airport rental cars. The first car he took was disabled and left behind after he drove it over the ground spikes. He then took a second car, drove it over the same spikes and made it out of the airport parking lot. I followed him here. The car is in the parking lot with flat tires. The male driver got out and walked over to the drive up window."

I said in a hungry, tired, and forced professional manner, after mumbling some unchoice words to myself, "Okay, let's go and you point him out to me."

So, with me hungrily leading the way and the guard walking right behind me, we approached the front entrance door. The guard shouted out, "That's him, that's him. He's coming in."

I said, "Okay." I looked at the suspect and then turned around to inform the guard of our apprehension plan. The guard was in full foot flight toward the back door in too much of a hurry. I said to myself, "Damn, this chump done stepped off and left me with no backup." So I, being an officer always on the prowl for a good arrest/nine zero eight-908, cautiously approached the suspect and began interviewing him about the involved vehicle in the parking lot, while trying to feel him out. The troublesome looking suspect had no intentions of being interviewed nor psyched. A struggle quickly ensued. We ended up wrestling on the floor. The manager rushed over and asked, "Officer do you need back up"?

I quickly and momentarily looked up at him and almost said, "What does it look like?" I then quickly changed my mind and said, "Yes." I had to be concerned about my free meal still on the table getting cold, while struggling in the front door and on the floor. I was a little relieved knowing that the assist officer call had gone out and the bruise brothers, (my bag, back, beg, bad), the brothers in blue were very fast en route. The first two officers on the scene happened to be The Fraternal Order of Police President and Vice President. This was during the time when they still had to work the streets. After they arrived, the suspect was eventually advised and arrested for a gun he had in his waistband. Lucky for him he didn't reach for it. He was also charged with auto theft (two counts), resisting arrest, and several warrants. I ended up doing all the paper work, including two tow reports and two vehicle theft reports. I also came upon the conclusion that the suspect had intended to rob the place. He couldn't drive the stolen car up to the drive thru window because of the flat tires. The cashier refused to open the drive up window because he wasn't driving, so he came inside with a gun and no money to place his order for cash. I later attempted to explain that fact finding situation to the police detectives, but they appeared to view it as an already signed, sealed, and delivered arrest with no further addressing needed. The security guard eventually came back after the action ended and the heat buildup from his rubber soles had dissipated. I even ate my cold breakfast before I went to the police station for a four hour day. The police internal affairs got involved after I submitted my overtime reports for two hours instead of the four I actually worked. They assumed I was working part time there and wasn't entitled to the adjusted over time pay. So they held up my over time pay for a long time, and I still don't know if I ever got it. This was after the manager and other workers gave statements that I wasn't working there before or after the above incident occurred. This was just another day's work for a hungry, tired, underpaid, overworked, over skilled, and under appreciated police officer trying to get his eat on and off.

POLICE SHOOTING (OFF DUTY)

I was involved in an off duty police shooting in front of 36 South 12th Street, Newark, New Jersey. The house was still being refurbished and my ex-girlfriend and I went there to look around because we had had prior break ins, and she was going back there to stay after dropping me off at my part time job. I was slowly walking toward the house because of a foot chase induced sprained ankle. Three males started running toward me hoping to get to me before I got into the house. I wasn't aware of this until later. I entered the house, leaving the outside entrance door partially open because I was coming right back. After inspecting the house, I started to leave. My ex-girlfriend, who was waiting for me in her car, started blowing her horn and yelling, "Watch out! Three guys are waiting on you." I pulled out my gun. Two of them immediately fled. The third one fled into the basement area. My ex-girlfriend, knowing I had a sprained ankle, jumped out of her car with part of her steering wheel lock. I took the lock from her and told her to go upstairs and request back up for the suspect still hiding in the basement. The suspect, apparently hearing this, came up out of the basement, and because of my bad ankle, he was able to get the steering lock from me and started assaulting his way completely out of the basement. I fired two shots hitting him in the lower leg. When that didn't stop him, I fired a third shot, which sent him sprawling onto the ground. The threat to my life was over. His wounds were not life threatening. I found out later he knew me, but didn't recognize me during the initial stages of the robbery attempt, and he took a plea in court. Internal affairs responded and assumed I shot the guy because I came home and caught him with my ex-girlfriend. She was shocked.

I said, "Don't be. The internal affairs lieutenant had downed a few as his breath forewarned, and he was only wildly speculating. He had just left another shooting involving a narcotics detective, who shot a suspect getting off a street telephone from a heated dispute and armed with a large caliber loaded handgun, and was probably tired. I initially thought my suspects were burglars and didn't know they had intended to knock my brains out and rob me. A lieutenant came by and asked me how many times I fired. I said, "Three."

After examining the stretched out suspect he said, "Good shooting. You hit him all three times." He left prior to the arrival of Internal Affairs. I was eventually cleared of any wrong doing involving that shooting.

HEAD SCRATCHING/GUN ARREST

This incident occurred while I was working off duty in uniform at one of my favorite, part time job locations on Elizabeth Avenue. I was standing outside in front of the restaurant that night making sure the parking lot was secure. A customer walked from the rear parking lot and secretively informed me that a male was circling the place in his car. "When he got in the rear, out of your sight, he brandished a gun and purposely scratched his head with it, and he looked as if he was looking for someone to hit up (shoot)." The customer then pointed out the vehicle and the suspect as the car made another tour.

I told the customer, "Okay, I got him." He walked away. I stood fast for a minute to keep the head scratching gun suspect from becoming suspicious, and I observed the gun in his hand from a rear window in the restaurant. I requested a back up unit, and I gave out a complete description of the car and a partial description of the suspect. I advised the dispatcher that he was armed and to have the responding police unit park at a specific location and wait for further instructions. The suspect eventually parked his vehicle on the corner of Hawthorne Avenue and Elizabeth Avenue eastbound, which meant his vehicle was facing the back up officer's vehicle, which was across the street. The suspect exited his vehicle and walked over to the pay telephone booth and used the telephone. I advised the dispatcher to have the back up police unit take him, with me providing cover. By the time that unit pulled across the width of Elizabeth Ave., the suspect, after observing them, got off the telephone, got into his idling car, backed up west on Hawthorne Ave., stopped and pulled up eastbound on Hawthorne Ave., made a left turn, northbound into the parking lot, where I was, and the police unit still hadn't crossed the street. I was standing in the parking lot, watching and saying, "Oh no, no. I can't let this become a wild car chase." This was one of those moments when there is no time to act or think. I ran out into the parking lot, positioning myself in front of the suspect's oncoming car with my gun drawn and ordered the suspect to stop his car. His front windows were down, so I knew it was no problem with him hearing me. My do or die plan was to jump onto or over his car if he continued moving toward me. The suspect complied by stopping his vehicle and he made moves as if he was removing the gun from his waist band and placing it under his seat while I was looking at him, and I held off squeezing off (firing). As he was concealing his weapon, the back up unit finally pulled up behind his vehicle and the others quickly jumped out. They ran over to the suspect's vehicle, ordered him out, frisked him and found nothing. They then, turned and looked at me with that "What's up" look. I holstered my gun, walked over and removed the loaded gun from under the driver's seat. The two back up officers, wristcuffed the prisoner, placed him in their late arriving car, took the evidence, the prisoner's car, and quickly left the scene.

When I later, reviewed their police reports for their version of what had happened, I was fortunate to have my name and my identification number in their report although I was the one who went to the grand jury. I'm still thanking those officers for the back up and glad that no one was injured even though The Head Scratching Gunman almost got away.

I THANK OUR DEAR LORD GOD

I thank Our Dear Lord God for
being Who He is, and there are
no greater words my heart and soul
could ever yield.

I thank Our Dear Lord God for
all He's done for all of humanity
I thank Our Dear Lord God for
His ever present presence.

I thank Our Dear Lord God for
the feeling of giving and receiving love.
I thank Our Dear Lord God for
the even greater thought of giving
and receiving the love stored for us in Heaven.

I thank Our Dear Lord God for
being our every living thing we'll ever need
I thank Our Dear Lord God for
turning empty space into eternity
in heaven for some of us.

I thank Our Dear Lord God for
His Son Jesus Christ and the happiness
that follows if we follow Him.

I thank Our Dear Lord God for
being The Greatest of all Greatness
and truly Our King of all Kings also
Our Lord of Lords and Our Perfect Unseen
Picture of Perfection.

Stay interested and—

CHECK YOUR CAP WEARING IQ'S

Say yo
Yo yo yeah u with the side wearing cap on your head and
U with the backwards wearing cap on your head.
Come over here.
Listen here,
Let's sit down at the round table and rap.

I don't know.
I'm kicking it to u.
Like I read it.

It's been said, your IQ's may be a reflection of how u wear
    your caps.
If u wanna be sideways gangsters,
Causing u to wear it sideways.
Cause your brains may be in sideways,
Causing u to sometimes talk out your faces sideways.
Causing u to sometimes walk sideways trying to follow your
    brim,
Causing your eyeballs to sometimes cross trying to locate
    your sideways brim,
Possible indications of your too much low IQ's.

I don't know.
I'm kicking it to u.
Like I read it.
Like I see it.

If u wanna be backward followers.
Causing u to wear it backwards,

Cause your brain may be in backwards,
Causing u to sometimes talk out your as- backwards,
Causing u to sometimes walk backwards trying to follow
    your brim,
Causing your eyeballs to sometimes roll backwards in your
    head, trying to hang with your brim,
Possible indications of a very low IQ.

I don't know.
I'm kicking it to u.
Like I read it.
Like I see it.
Like I hear it.

If u wanna be straight leaders,
Causing u to wear it straight,
Cause your brain maybe in straight,
Causing u to sometimes talk straight up,
Causing u to sometimes walk and act straight, trying to
    follow your brim,
Causing your eyes to concentrate on what's straight out in
    front of your brim,
Possible indications of a very high IQ.

I don't know.
I'm kicking it to u straight up/on.
Like I read it.
Like I see it.
Like I hear it.
Like I feel it.
Like I wear it.

I don't know.
What do u know?
Check your lids.

The ones that cover your brains that may reflect the answers
    to your IQ's
 reflect the answers to your IQ's
the answers to your IQ's
answers to your IQ's
to your IQ's
your IQ's
IQ's

(Important Questions/IQ's, Important Answers/IA's should
be what we're more concerned about)

CHAPTER VI

THE SLEEPERS BEWARE

The following incidents are being placed in a category entitled "Sleepers." The involved folks/suspects were apprehended as a result of being initially asleep.

This incident occurred as Police Officer "Wild Bill" of the famed South District Police Station and I were on Lyons Ave. near Parkview Terrace. We observed a double parked vehicle, and upon investigating the circumstances surrounding the vehicle, we found the vehicle to be occupied by a lone sleeping front seat male passenger. While trying to awaken him, a plastic bag containing marijuana was recovered from his person and the sleeping non-beauty was arrested. The feeling and sound of the wristcuffs being placed on his wrists brought him completely around out of his deep sleep. While we were involved with him, the driver and owner of the involved vehicle came out of a house. He, while spitting out verbal salads (profanity), demanded an explanation. While Wild Bill was trying to advise him of the circumstances surrounding the arrest, I continued to look over the vehicle and discovered a handgun protruding from beneath the driver's front seat. After the weapon was recovered and neither man could produce a permit, they were both arrested. It's my contention the driver/owner initially observed what was going on from a distance before he approached the vehicle. He probably thought his man was going down (being arrested) for the gun, which was probably his and didn't know he (his passenger) had drugs on him. He would've probably stayed back and waited to see if his vehicle would be towed if he knew the initial arrest was for the drugs. He approached because he didn't want his man to go down for probably his gun alone and he didn't—they both went.

The bottom, middle, and top line is that a crime/accident scene search is never completed because you may never find out what was left behind.

To touch on crime scenes, my last partner, Big Brit, and I helped handle a motorcycle accident involving a fatality. The deceased and his motorcycle impacted a car and he then impacted a pole. The impact caused his cellular telephone to sail from his waistband and land almost a block away. Crime/accidents scenes may have no boundaries.

Another incident involving Big Brit and myself occurred when we responded to a robbery report on Clinton Ave. The victim, an elderly security guard, was mugged/robbed for his wallet that contained cash. A struggle ensued and the victim bit off a piece of his assailant's ear. After we arrived, the victim looked like a vampire with the suspect's blood all around his mouth. The victim was cleaned up and a good crime scene search was conducted. After prying information from the victim, the ear piece was recovered. The suspect was eventually found at the hospital by our field lieutenant. We responded and arrested the suspect as he questioned one of the doctors as to how long would take for his missing ear piece to grow back. The doctors told him it wouldn't grow back and they couldn't reattach the piece that was bitten off. The security guard not only ended up with a mouth full of blood, but he ended up losing his job. The incident occurred across the street from where he once worked.

The Second Sleeper

This incident unfolded as another one of my partners and I were working together in uniform on the evening shift assigned to a marked police vehicle. We were dispatched to an assignment in the upper Weequahic Section to investigate a male suspect sleeping in a car and blocking a driveway. While en route to the assignment, we were given additional information. No one was at the home of the blocked driveway. Also, the caller didn't recognize the idling car nor the operator behind the wheel. After arriving at that location, the involved vehicle's registration was checked via the dispatcher while the operator was still breathing and asleep. The vehicle check came back as a properly registered vehicle with no stop notices attached. The operator was eventually awakened and asked out of the vehicle. The registration check showed it was registered to an older female. He slowly and sleepily complied. He was then asked for his driver's license, vehicle registration, and vehicle insurance card. He slowly and hesitantly removed his wallet and said, "Everything is in there," While trying to distract me as he handed over his wallet, he removed a small brown paper bag from his front pant's pocket. I knocked his hand with the wallet away from me, knocking the wallet from his grasp. He took that opportunity to toss the brown bag. My partner, by now realizing something was up or about to go down, detained the suspect. I went to retrieve the tossed bag, and the suspect took that opportunity to jerk his way free and run away aided by the darkness. At that time, I wasn't aware my partner had a bad ticker and couldn't run. The tossed bag was recovered, along with the suspect's wallet. The bag contained several tin foils of cocaine. The wallet had the suspect's name, address, social security number, date of birth, even his mother's name and address. It turned out the car was registered to his mother. The vehicle was towed, traffic summonses issued, the drugs and other reports were submitted. A warrant was issued for the suspect's arrest, although his main concern was probably an explanation to his mother concerning the whereabouts of her car.

The kicker to this is to have a partner with a good ticker. Also, watch out for those "Sleepers" who may end up putting you to sleep.

THE THIRD SLEEPER

This incident occurred while I was working off duty and in full police uniform at a restaurant on Elizabeth Avenue. It was on a weekend, between 4 and 5 a.m. The jammed parking lot crowd was starting to thin out. Vehicles had been doubled and tripled parked. The stomach filled motorists were slowly leaving, snaking their way around and out of the lot. My attention was then drawn to this one idling doubled parked vehicle. It looked odd and stood out because most of the other vehicles parked near it had pulled out. I was standing in the lot thinking to myself, "Should I approach the vehicle and call in a vehicle registration check or will it soon be gone just like the other vehicles?" While still in this contemplating mode, a two officer, marked police vehicle called the police dispatcher and requested a p.a. (police action) and the request indicated the officers would be at my exact same location for crowd control. So I said, "Good that's the answer to my question. They were reading my mind, and I'll wait for them before taking any action."

Approximately fifteen minutes went by and no police. Apparently the officers placed themselves at my location and went else where. Being a veteran officer and with an understanding of these situations, I decided to get the officers to my location and cover for them at the same time. I called the dispatcher on my portable police radio and requested the police unit that took the p.a. at this location pull around from the front side of our location and assist me in the rear of the parking lot with a vehicle stop as if they were already there. Before the dispatcher could relay that request, the officers in that police unit cut in and stated, "Tell that off duty man, we're pulling around now." They were probably in Elizabeth, New Jersey. Those officers peeled into the lot in a matter of a few short minutes with their emergency lights blaring, pulled up to me and excitedly asked, "What you got fam (short for family)?"

I said, "Thanks. I got an unlawfully parked vehicle with no front license plate, an expired inspection sticker, and two, sleeping, male occupants, one in the right front seat and the other in the right rear seat."

We approached the vehicle while the two breathing gents slept and checked the vehicle's registration via the dispatcher. The registration came back registered to another vehicle, and the two males were awakened, frisked ,and asked to sit in the police vehicle for a field interview and a further check of the vehicle's identification number (VIN). While this was taking place, I walked around the vehicle looking for whatever I could see, remembering the captain's advice to observe with no blinders on. I observed a 9 millimeter handgun protruding from beneath the driver's front seat. The two passengers were advised of their rights and arrested. They continually denied any knowledge of the gun, the driver, the owner of the vehicle, how they got there, or why they were still there. They didn't know anything. The right front seat passenger stated, "All I remember is I had been drinking and got picked up from my girl's house."

I asked him for his girl's telephone number. Maybe she'll remember who the driver was.

He said, "I don't know it by heart."

I then asked him, "What about from memory? What does your heart have to do with you remembering anything?"

He laughed without providing an answer. I believe the driver was on the pay telephone on the corner, talking during the entire episode, that conversation for whatever it was worth, caused him the car and the arrest of his two friends, although I had no proof. Unfortunately for those passengers, they got arrested for the gun and open outstanding warrants. Fortunately, for me, those officers took that late arriving p.a., and I waited for them. Thanks again officers.Good Job.

Hip pocket info for all police officers: Be where you are suppose to be in a timely manner, and be aware of the "Sleepers."

MAY WE THANK OUR LORD, YES

May we say with our mouths, how much we love Our Lord

May **we** pay with the love in our hearts, what we owe Him for being Our Lord

May each day we **thank** Him for being Who He Is, Our Lord

May our way be paved in The Footsteps of **Our Lord**

May the jay birds in their splendor, chirp in harmony with us and our songs of Our Lord

May we lay as well as pray, as we think on and of Our Lord

May His ray of sunlight continue to provide enlightenment, as we forever obey Our Lord

May a bay in galloping stride reach his destination, as we stride to reach Our Lord

AND, DEAR LORD, WE THANK YOU FOR THE OPPORTUNITY TO THANK YOU

Stay Interested——

A LOVE SONG

Female Vocal
I'm lying here in the sand,
Tanning and planning
How to make u my man

Male Vocal
You're super fresh,
You're fresh.

Female Vocal
Everything I do leaves me
Chilling , illing, and feeling u.

Male Vocal
All you're super cool,
You're cool

Female Vocal
Baby, let me right
All your wrongs.

Male Vocal
You're super smart,
You're smart.

Female Vocal
I'll run from here to eternity and back,

Before you'll lose any thought of me.

Male Vocal
All you're super quick,
You're quick.

Female Vocal
U won't make it a fight,
Which would be so delight.

Male Vocal
You're super tough,
You're tough.

Female Vocal
No, No, No, I'm super hot,
I'm hot.

Male Vocal
Ok baby listen
Listen to my heart beat a love tune to u
Listen to my heart pulsate love messages to u
Listen to my heart rhythms
Send out love rhymes to u

And if u didn't here it, then listen
Listen to my heart pound out love notes to u,
Listen to my heart pulsate love messages to u,
Listen to my heart rhythms,

Send out A Love Song to you.
Just listen to my heart,
Listen to my heart,
Listen to my heart sing out I love u,
Listen to my heart sing never too much I love u,
Listen to my heart sing,
Twenty four/seven I love u.

CHAPTER VII

THE DOBERMAN PINSCHER GANG

This incident fell into the above category due to the above named dogs, once a feared and very popular breed. Pit bulls and Rottweilers, in my opinion, have since replaced them. This incident started out as a run of the mill drug arrest on Astor Street. My partner Fitz and I were working the day shift (0800-1600 hours) in uniform and in a marked police vehicle. We arrested a well known, tall, slim, dark skinned suspect for the unlawful possession of drugs. The suspect, who still frequents that area today, at one time was very athletic with good hand skills. My partner and I ran up on him in the hallway and this was one of those situations I cherished. He couldn't get around, under, or run over us, at least for the moment. He calmly submitted to the arrest and was wristcuffed from behind, searched, and led out of the drug troublesome hallway. I was behind him and my partner was in the front, leading and looking like Sinatra with his police hat cocked to the side. The prisoner made a sudden dash, getting past my partner with scantily dressed ladies of the evening in the hallway providing the distraction and one of them screaming for him not to run. The prisoner hit the first entrance door with his shoulder and leaped off the steps, hit the final entrance door with another strong shoulder move and was outside. He ran west on Astor Street, all the while still wristcuffed from behind, then south on Brunswick Street and up to a fence with several Doberman Pinschers on the other side, looking hungry, which is where I caught up to him.

My partner, after making sure the "ladies" were okay, got into our police vehicle and was waiting for the prisoner on Sherman Avenue, the other side of the fence. After catching up to the prisoner, who was jumping around like a kick boxer and looking for an undecided out, I, instead of wrestling him down to the ground, tried to knock him down with a wild leaping left hook, which was the counter for his foot work. The prisoner, with a lot of athleticism still left, slipped my over zealous punch and I hit the dirt hard on my face from the forceful momentum of the thrown and missed slug. The prisoner, aware of and nearly on the receiving end of my desperation, backed up from the fence got a running start and leaped over the four foot fence, head and chest first, and took his chances with the dogs. You would think he became dog meat— no. Unbelievingly, the dogs ignored him and started barking, snarling, and growling at me, keeping me at bay which allowed the prisoner to get up off his face and start running through the yard. I ducked down and hid, hoping to play fake him out, getting him to think I ran to the other side so he would run back toward me and releap back into my arms for a second take down chance. He couldn't be played and continued running through the yard. I wasn't taking any chances going in that yard with the dogs. After being thoroughly embarrassed, back up officers were requested. All I remember my partner repeatedly saying, "He's a bad man, he's a bad man." We didn't tell the back up officers over the air waves that the prisoner was wristcuffed. They were told verbally as they arrived on the scene. The dispatcher was thinking we were looking for a suspect and not a prisoner.

A thorough search was conducted on the perimeters of the Doberman's gang house. No one had yet decided when or how we would enter the yard. In the mean time, the freedom seeking prisoner had somehow desperately slipped passed us and made it to a friend's apartment, a couple of doors away. The responding sergeant and his chauffeur developed information as to the prisoner's whereabouts. They located the prisoner in a nearby friend's room, and he was rearrested and additionally charged with resisting arrest. The prisoner appeared to be a little relieved he was found by the sergeant and not by my partner or myself. Since there was no mention over the air waves of a prisoner escaping, only a suspect on the run, the good sergeant, for the sake of the good old times, let us off that one (departmental charges). Oh, by the way, the sergeant was the same supervisor, that located the suspect in University Hospital, who had a piece of his ear bitten off by the victim. Excellent work lieutenant, his present rank and thanks again. Prisoners can and will run at any time, in any situation and no matter what their chances are of getting away.

This following incident fell in under the Doberman pinscher gang category, simply because it involved an incident involving some other Dobermans. My partner, The Rev, The Preacher, and myself, Buck, were working together in uniform and in a marked police vehicle. We were dispatched to see a female complainant in reference to a partially stripped reported stolen car in her rear yard. Prior to making contact with the complainant, concerned neighbors approached us on our arrival and informed us that the complainant's grandson was the culprit. They further stated he drove the stolen car into his grandmother's rear yard and stripped it. The whole neighborhood knew what he did. Besides that, they told the grandmother to call the police to get the car towed. After finally locating and then conferring with the complainant, the grandmother, we informed her of the information we had developed concerning the stolen car and her grandson, who she initially said wasn't home. Her adult grandson apparently was home and overheard us talking, and slipped out of the house. He climbed a neighbor's fence and hid in her Dobermans's dog house. As a result of hurriedly ascending to the top and over the fence, he ripped a gash in his testicles and was bleeding. The thought of lost blood and him becoming fresh bloody dog meat was running rampant through his mind. What was running even more rampant, important, and fresh on his mind was getting treatment for his wound. While he was in the dog house thinking, my partner and I conducted a search of the house and outside, all around the fenced-in, prancing, barking, and charging Dobermans. After thinking the suspect was long gone, we went back into the house to wait for the tow truck. Sharper police officers would've checked the top of that fence and secured that valuable evidence—small bloody pieces of clothing and even smaller pieces human flesh—that we missed.

The bleeding suspect, tired of trying to apply pressure to his testicles to stop the bleeding, waved off the anti-police Dobermans and reclimbed the fence. He slipped back into the house for some immediate treatment and got some gauze from the medicine cabinet, and this time he went into the attic crawl space to hide. With his testicles being in the shape that they were in, the suspect made a lot of unintentional noise trying to gingerly crawl along.

My partner, I, and his grandmother went up to the attic to investigate and shortly thereafter, we ordered the suspect to come out. Being overly concerned about his testicles, he came out and informed us of his medical needs. We immediately requested an ambulance. The suspect, while waiting for the ambulance, admitted driving the stolen car home, partially stripping it, and placing the stolen parts in a padlocked room in the basement. The prisoner insisted on us taking him to the hospital or calling him a cab. He felt the ambulance was taking much too long, and he was overly concerned about what he called his "nuts." We transported him to the hospital where he was put into even more pain while receiving several sutures while he was awake.

After he was released, he was arrested for possession of stolen property. Unfortunately for him, he slit his testicles. Fortunately for us, he did or he would've stayed in that doghouse and wouldn't have been caught that day. Imagine if it would've have been a cathouse; he would've never come out.

OUR LORD

Joyful songs, honoring the glory of **our
Lord**, is a delight
Meanful prayer thanking **Our Lord** for who **He** is every
    night
Maintaining positive faith is within sight

At first light,
At last twilight.

Meanful fasting is as sunlight,
Is to all life in flight,
On the ground, to our left or right.

To b-right
Is being bright.

Let your brightful, delightful ways be seen in **Our Lord's**
    light
And under **Our Lord's** might,
Every day and tonight.

CHAPTER VIII

BELIEVE IT OR NOT

This incident occurred in The Newark Police 5th Precinct/ South District Station area back in 1971. A police car, parked on Clinton Ave., was occupied by two police officers, the driver and the passenger (observer). While seated in their vehicle, doing whatever they were doing, a female came frantically running toward their police car screaming, yelling, using profanity and acting in a total belligerent manner. The young and quick acting observer took out his gun and shot her. I'm assuming he thought he was under a direct attack and feared for his life. His partner, the driver, typed all of the police reports and eventually got his partner cleared. I think the partner missed his calling and should've been an attorney.

The female was eventually taken to the hospital via an ambulance. Her story was that she approached the police car in the manner she did because she was running for her life from an ensuing male attacker. That impending butt beating caused her to get shot. I don't believe she ever filed a complaint against the officer nor against whoever was chasing her. The gun shot wasn't life threatening and I believe she checked herself out of the hospital before the investigation was complete or before she could be thoroughly questioned.

This incident wasn't mentioned to bring back bad memories or bygones. It's being mentioned to let everyone know it did happen and can happen again. STAY ALERT AND STAY ALIVE. The above observer eventually left the department years ago for personal reasons and the driver had a long successful career and retired.

KNOW YOUR PARTNER'S OBVIOUS CAPABILITIES

This incident occurred as an unnamed police officer, my partner at the time, and I were assigned in uniform to a foot patrol post on the evening shift on Bergen Street. I had already established myself as an aggressive, hard working cop, and my partner was rumored to be more than uninterested, lazy, and very careless. I don't know if my supervisors assigned us together on purpose or by accident. Maybe they wanted me to have an easy tour, show my partner some For-Real police work or have both of us end up getting drummed up. So as the quiet, uneventful evening wore on we received a dispatched call to respond to an area between Renner Avenue and Custer Avenue on Bergen Street. The call was in reference to four to five males involved in drug activity with a dispute. As we arrived in the area on foot we observed the above males near Custer Avenue acting suspicious, and the dispatcher was informed. We approached them and asked them to assume the position against a wall while explaining to them the nature of our actions. My partner performed the frisks while I provided cover, the first frisk was a bull s—(wasted) frisk, and my partner told that suspect to leave. The suspect replied, "Thank you, officer, have a nice evening," and started walking off.

I said, "Hold up a second. Step over here."

The suspect suspiciously said, "For what? Your partner already checked me."

I said, "Yeah, I know, and I'm checking you again."
My partner even stated, "Al, he's clean,"
I remained visibly locked on the suspect who appeared to look cross eyed and much too scared. He pretended to ignore me and attempted to walk off. I reached out, grabbed him, and got him to understand who was in charge. In the interim, my partner quickly frisked the other suspects and sent them on their way. I conducted a refrisk on the first suspect and removed a loaded handgun from his waist band. He was abruptly placed on the ground for crime scene control, thoroughly searched and arrested. Needless to say, my partner had nothing to say at that point or for the remainder of the tour. He realized then he had let an obviously armed suspect almost walk. It was completely obvious to the feel, the naked eye, or to someone wearing corrective lens. Even a blind man with no hands would've known the suspect was armed. Always try to get to know your partner's OBVIOUS CAPABILITIES whether it be his being aggressive, slow, strong, weak, fast, disinterested, accurate, or whatever they may be. It may be in your best interest as to whether you return HOME, to HEAVEN or to HELL, and I'm being really being for real.

THE LOU

This incident occurred in the South District Police Station a while back. A lieutenant about 6'5" tall and weighing from 300-350 lbs. was working as the Desk Lieutenant. Two police officers brought in a wristcuffed prisoner and informed the lieutenant of his charges. The prisoner started spitting, not rapping or saliva, but verbal salads (profanity) which began to irritate the lieutenant. It irritated him to the point he flew (ran very fast) from behind the desk and confronted the prisoner. they both began spitting verbal salads at each other. The two arresting officers had positioned themselves to either side of the prisoner and slightly to the rear in preparation for any confrontation. The angry prisoner apparently bumped the lieutenant who was already highly agitated. The lieutenant retaliated by throwing a punch at the prisoner. The big and agile prisoner slipped it causing the lieutenant to miss. With his weight and forward momentum, he hit the floor face first. The sound of the big lieutenant crashing to the floor brought officers from all over the station to the area. They were yelling, "What happen? He knocked the Lou down! He knocked the Lou down!" Someone answered, "No, he's cuffed." Other officers kept screaming, "The Lou is down! The Lou is out!"

The now silent prisoner was eventually ushered into a cell for his own safety until it was completely understood by everyone what had actually happened. The lieutenant threw a punch, missed and fell on his face. He was eventually helped to his feet, uninjured and totally embarrassed. It was very hard for the lieutenant to forget that one. As a young officer, he was an excellent and very aggressive cop. He and his partner brought in two to three arrest every day. The good, big jolly fellow is happily, standing tall and retired.

OFF DUTY

This incident occurred one evening as I was working off duty, part time, and in regular clothes in Black's, a store on the corner of Hawthorne Ave. and Leslie St. This one customer came in, who I previously knew from walking the beat on Bergen St. I arrested him a couple of times in the past. He was one of those long term drug users. After entering the store and making a purchase, he said in a friendly manner, "How long have you been working here?"

I replied with, "A minute (which is short for not long)."

He replied with, "I hope you didn't get caught up in those lay offs." The City of Newark was, at the time, laying employees off.

While trying to anticipate his motive, because he never held a conversation with me before, I lied and said, "Yeah, I got laid off."

He looked up at me in a very odd and peculiar manner and said, "You punk as- (m/f), I oughta beat your sorry as-. What time you git the (f) off?"

I, while shocked and not believing what I just heard said, "10 p.m."

He came back with, "Bet I'll be here, and I'm stepping to your punk as-," while walking out of the store and firmly grasping his private parts. So, just before we closed, I got mentally and physically prepared, with some light shadow boxing, prepared to knock this joker out. I honestly believed he was coming back, knowing him like I did. Apparently someone must have pulled his coat in the interim and informed him of the real deal, that I wasn't laid off. I didn't see him that night or for some time after that. When I did finally run into him, all I got was a lot of "yes" and "no sirs." Some criminals are always watching your moves and waiting. It's imperative for police officers wherever they may be to stay alert and alive.

HERE'S YOUR DOG

There was once a low level drug user and dealer known as Bull Dog, who I got to know very well and eventually arrested. He was given the street name Bull Dog by his family and friends, because his face actually resembled a bull dog's. He peddled his wares in the area of Hawthorne Avenue, back in the late 1970s and early 1980s. This was during the time, the drug dealing circles began to get over crowded. A lot of drug dealers and runners got run out and had to turn to other criminal activity else where. So Bull Dog ran out, eventually ran down on and robbed a slightly higher level drug dealer at gun point. He took the fruits of the robbery, money and drugs, and fled the area. He ended up not too far away in a now long gone bar on Avon Avenue and Ridgewood Avenue, an area later to be known as the Fish Bowl. He unfortunately ran into an off duty cop, now long retired, in the bar. The cop happened to be exercising his hand, wrist, forearm, elbow, and mouth, attempting to satisfy a big thirst. He blindly looked over and observed Bull Dog. Using his street smarts sense, it was obvious that the sweating and scared Bull Dog, looking around, had just done some wrong. He tactfully approached Bull Dog. After a brief verbal and slight physical confrontation, he relieved Bull Dog of some stickup money, drugs, and a bulging gun, then sent him scampering on his way. Bull Dog didn't even get a chance to count the money or sniff the drugs. Bull Dog eventually further paid for his dogged day afternoon by getting hit up/shot five times, from the waist down for the unauthorized robbery. Back in those days, when a hit was put out on you, they didn't try to kill you. The hit men just tried to cripple you, so that you and others wouldn't ever forget why you got shot. They figured if you're dead, others would quickly forget you and you wouldn't be here to suffer or remember anything.

Today, they shoot and try to kill the intended target, and anybody else that may happen to be around. I was on foot patrol on Bergen St. and actually observed Bull Dog in the back of a police car being rushed to the hospital on Lyons Avenue after he was shot. So, it was the police, who Bull Dog was always on the run from, that he eventually had to run to after getting shot, and they helped save his life. Being the prowling Bull Dog he was, he recovered and continued his bull dogged criminal activity. Sometime after being shot, and while still recovering with the use of a cane, my partner and I saw him walking east on Hawthorne Ave. near Bergen Street. We didn't notice the two plain clothes officers from The Essex County Sheriff's Department, also quickly walking behind him that same evening. Until they called out to him, he looked back, tossed his cane and stepped off, fleeing east on Hawthorne Ave., with the officers in slow pursuit. It took the speed of my partner, after exiting our vehicle, to run him down, and he was turned over to the sheriff's officers. Bull Dog is no longer with us. He's patiently waiting for his life long entrance into hell if he left here unrepentant.

The above incident was not mentioned to dig up, deep down and long gones. It was mentioned because it happened and will probably, somewhere, happen again. By the way young officers, beware of any drug dealers, runners, or players that happen to act or look like a dog. Most of them cats (another word for fellows back in the 1960s) are pussies, no matter how they act or look.

LOVE

God is love
And all He created is the true face of love.

God's beautiful and ever lasting love
Will be brought to unmatched light
As effortlessly as a beautiful dove
In unmatched flight.

And all its consuming wing span of beauty,
God's angels will consume an even greater airspace of
beauty.

Dear Lord, thank You for Your patience and unending love
Dear Lord, thank You for allowing me to say these things
from all of my heart, which is a gift of Your never ending
love.

From You, Dear Lord to me and all others with a beautiful
desire to love
To You, Dear Lord from me and all others with a beautiful
desire to forever honor and receive Your beautiful love.

Which is a never ending generous love,

The cross Your son died on will always bear Your forever
shown love.

A Song for All Seasons

A WARMER LOVE

When I'm in your arms,
I find a wonderful warm feeling of love, love in my heart.

I never wanna FALL out of your gentle caresses, except
Only to fall further in love, in love with you, in a warmer
     love with you.

There's so much SPRING in your kisses,
They make me wanna kiss and hold onto you forever and
     ever.
All when I'm in your arms

And in the WINTER time,
I find plenty of SUMMER time.
When I'm near you and your wonderful warmer love,
I can see your love eyes glowing with love confirming our
Love being the corner stone of our togetherness.
All when I'm in your arms.

In the Summer, June will have its warmer way.
In the Spring, March will have her flowered days.
In the Fall, September will flutter the bays.
In the Winter, chilly old man December will have his say.

No matter what the season,
Let's have our love say our love way, our love days at our
     love bays.
And have an all season love in
Right here and now, especially

When I hear your warm lips, whisper a warmer, I love you.
When I feel your warm caress, warm me
Through and through,
Day and night,
I know then
It's a wonderful warmer love, all season long, all season
   long.
All when I'm in your arms, all when I'm in your warm arms.

CHAPTER IX

BRIT AND ONE OF HIS PARTNERS

It's only fitting to end this book as I ended my wonderful, long career with only a few down moments with episodes of Brit, my last partner. Brit and I went on call for a missing child report. We located the child, prior to the report being taken. While at the lady's house, I noticed a picture on her wall of Richard L. Allen, the founder of The First African Methodist Episcopal Church in America and I pointed it out to Brit, when you see him Newark, New Jersey officers, ask him what he said.

Too Much Strong Brit and Too Much Poor Rich

Brit and I were assigned to a walking beat on Avon Avenue, between South 10th Street and South 20th Street. We were given a police vehicle to expedite our patrol coverage. We stopped a motorist on South 12th Street and Avon Avenue for a motor vehicle violation. Brit approached the driver, the only occupant, and I approached the right side of the vehicle. I was very discreet in my approach, and the driver thought Brit was alone. There was some question, concerning the driver's driving credentials, so Brit asked him out of his car. In the mean time, I was still unnoticed by the driver, I looked into the passenger's side window and observed a gun protruding from beneath the passenger's front seat. While the driver was out of the vehicle and his back to me, I opened the passenger's door and removed the loaded gun. I held the gun up high enough for Brit to see it, and he nodded in an affirmative manner. He asked the driver if he had a permit for a gun. The driver made two powerful looking fists and said, "I don't need a permit for these. I was born with them." He had a horrible odor of cat hit (alcoholic beverage) on his breath. Brit spun the man around and up against his car and wristcuffed him, which is when the man first observed me and almost tripped over his lower lip as his cat hit mouth had dropped open.

Too Much Brit And Not Enough Rich

Brit and I was in a marked police vehicle on patrol, we happen to be on Jelliff Ave. and Avon Ave., just outside of the Fish Bowl. When we pulled another vehicle over for a motor vehicle violation. Brit had the sharpest eyes for delinquent inspection stickers and missing front plates of any of the previous officers I've worked with. After pulling this vehicle over, I went to the driver's side and Brit to the passenger side. There were three occupants in the vehicle, the right rear seat passenger had a cast on his leg and the front seat passenger was a female, the rear seat passenger's girlfriend. The possibility of chasing three people had decreased to one, the driver. With that in mind, as I asked the driver to exit the vehicle for being unlicensed. While he was feeling his pockets, trying to make a driver's license appear out of nowhere. He pulled out a can of soda and asked me to hold it for him, while pretending to check his other pockets for the driver's license. He hadn't pulled this trick out of thin air, and the soda can ended up on the ground. The sucker move was for me to reach for the soda and that would've had been the second of distraction, he needed for freedom. I was so close to him, he couldn't swing and he wasn't big enough to run me over. After my instincts took over, I put him up against the car and removed a loaded 9 mm handgun from his waistband. He was arrested, the other two people were interviewed by robbery squad detectives and released. What was about to take place, is that the rear seat passenger on crutches had been shot earlier, in a nearby housing area called the little bricks/low income housing. They were in the area for a pay back visit, until we rode by on a disrupt unwelcome visit.

DALLAS STRONG MAN BRIT AND GIANTS ALMOST STRONG MAN RICH

Our police station roll call was just over with, and Brit was anxiously waiting in the marked police vehicle for me to exit the police station. I finally came out and got in our vehicle and Brit said he was going to try and catch up with a sports utility vehicle that had driven past the station with a defective tail light. We caught up with the vehicle on Hunterdon St. and Clinton Ave. With the use of our emergency lights and siren, the SUV was pulled over. I exited our vehicle and when I approached the SUV, the driver slightly lowered the window. I, from a distance, asked him for his driver's license, registration and insurance card. The driver dropped the gear shift in low and pulled off while I remained standing in the middle of the street. Brit had been repositioning the police vehicle behind the SUV. I ran back to our vehicle. The SUV traveled north on Hunterdon St., ran the stop (**S**tate **T**rooper **O**n **P**atrol-**S**tate **T**ax **O**n **P**eople) sign and smashed into a vehicle that had been traveling east on Madison Ave. The SUV flipped over at least twice. If you would've seen what we ssw, you would never own a SUV. Two suspects crawled out. Brit went after the driver and caught him a couple blocks away. I remained at the scene and summoned medical attention for the driver of the east bound vehicle and called for back up. The second suspect was apprehended by back up officers. The two suspects were treated for accident related injuries and arrested for possession of a stolen vehicle. The other motorist survived, only because, he was traveling in an old sturdy car.

BRIT AND RICH

Brit was my last partner. He said, " I hate to see you leave." I actually hated to leave, but if I hadn't left, I wouldn't be writing this book.

Brit and I handled this particular assignment just before I retired. This assignment should serve as an eye opener for new officers. They have to be prepared and alert on all assignments, no matter how low of a priority the assignment may be. Dispatchers used to give out what they considered drive by assignments because of the dust that was on them and their low priority. That so called drive by assignment is going to cause some officer unwanted problems in the future.

This assigment that Brit and I handled wasn't considered a drive by at the time, but it fit the category because the caller had been waiting for a police car for a while. It was an unwanted guest call. A female rooming house tenant, who had moved, returned to get one suitcase and became unruly. The landlord called the police. We responded and met him near the corner of Lyons Ave. and Aldine St. He explained to us that the involved roomer had moved and had returned to pick up a suitcase he allowed her to leave behind, but she became belligerent. All he wanted her to do was to leave. The landlord escorted us to the room and knocked on the door. The female, not knowing we were there, snatched opened the door. The landlord walked in and invited us in, pointing out the problem female. I walked in the room first and Brit second. This always had a psychological effect since Brit was taller and more muscular. I observed a male to my left with a large gun in his hands. He sprung around in an attempt to conceal the weapon and placed it in his clothing.

I pulled out my weapon and yelled, "He's got a gun."

Brit pulled out his weapon and ordered the rather large suspect, who weighed at least 300 lbs. and was 6'5" tall, up against the wall and to his knees. He had to bring him down to size. The gun was removed from the suspect, and it was discovered that he had no permit. He was eventually advised and arrested. As you read, this started out as a dispute and ended with another party with a gun.

After leaving that location and arriving at robbery squad with the prisoner, I discovered I left my prescription eye glasses at the scene. Brit went back to the scene and discovered the landlord had been thoroughly assaulted by the prisoner's brothers and friends. He repeatedly refused a written report or any medical attention. He was lumped up ugly bad. He stated the suspects stopped the beat down after he kept yelling out that he had called the police on the female and didn't know she had anyone else in the room. After the landlord continued to refuse any assistance, Brit rendered first aid, requested an ambulance for him, and then inquired about my eyeglasses. The landlord and others who entered the room after we left denied any knowledge of the glasses. some of them even claimed I didn't wear glasses. Brit eventually remembered that money talks and everything else walks. He went into his slide and pulled out a $10 bill, offering it as a reward. He was also thinking that if I couldn't see, he would have to do all of the typing.

One of the males, who never took his eyes off of that ten spot, told Brit, "Hold on to that, I'll be right back. Let me check with this other brother that was here and left." He came running back with my eye glasses and got paid. Brit returned to robbery squad and informed me of his unexpected expenditure. His loss caused me to kick out a Hamilton in repaying him. My get even plans were already being master planned. We went back to that location several times in the following months for fair and friendly minded police business, which resulted in two separate drug possession arrests. I've happily left that entire area in Brit's capable and safe hands.

Brit was big, strong, athletic, and he could run. His mere presence helped us to stay out of Internal Affairs many times. I would've given him a run for his money fifteen years ago with my stop and go, spinning, hesitation, left handed hook shot, in the paint, but he came along much too late, and at my age now, he's probably got a defense for that shot, although I might just find out.

BRIT AND OUR SMOKING GUN ARREST

This incident occurred as my last partner and I were en route to the South District Police Station with a prisoner wanted on warrants. While traveling in our marked police vehicle, north on Bergen St., crossing Custer Ave., we heard several gun shots. The correct course of action was to notify the dispatcher and continue on to the police station with our prisoner as long as the shots weren't being fired in our presence and no one required any medical attention. We did quite the opposite, being overly concerned about our citizenry. We notified the dispatcher and went back. We made a u turn on Bergen St., a left turn onto Custer Ave., traveling east toward Hunterdon St. At that intersection, we observed three belligerent males in each other's faces beefing(arguing). One of them had a gun, but he tossed it after he noticed us. He didn't think we saw the toss move. Brit quickly exited our vehicle and ordered all three surprised men on the ground face first while I covered him. Our hands were full. We had those three males and the one in the rear of our vehicle wristcuffed. We had to gain and maintain control of the situation quickly. After the three men were neatly spread eagled on the ground and our prisoner was still intact, I went over to the nearby hedges where the gun had been tossed and retrieved it still warm and smoking. The suspect who tossed it was arrested for the unlawful possession of a gun. The other two were frisked, advised, told they were lucky, and sent on their way. Another unlawful gun off the streets of Newark, N.J. and conscientious officers going far beyond the numerous calls and answers to duty.

CRIME FIGHTERS DISPENSING MORE THAN JUST ICE

This particular on duty incident involving my partner Brit and myself. We were ordered by our lieutenant to the area of Watson Ave. and Hillside Ave. We were sent there to investigate a strenuous complaint of drug activity emanating from the only apartment building on the short block. We were also told to detain any suspicious characters for an interview and to notify him concerning any interviews.

After arriving at the above location, we checked the front and rear. We then entered the unlocked front entrance door and performed a vertical patrol on the interior, the stairs and hallways. On the way down from the upper floors, we encountered a rather large male suspect in the first floor hall, acting suspicious as if he was looking for us or our vehicle. We had parked our marked police vehicle around the corner to prevent forewarning any obvious suspects. The adult suspect in the hall didn't have any identification, wasn't sure of his name or where he lived, so we notified the lieutenant. The lieutenant responded to the scene along with two detectives and began to interview the suspect. He insisted on the interview being done in his apartment because he had two young children in there he was concerned about. The detectives, the suspect, and I entered his apartment, and after making sure the two children were okay, the interview continued. The suspect nervously worked his way over to where a video cassette recorder tape case was lying, picked it up, and tried to insert it into the rear of his waistband while verbally b/s his way through the interview. I approached him and asked him, "What are you doing?"

The struggle was on. He and his three hundred pounds plus were no final match for the two detectives and myself. We over powered him, removed the VCR case, opened it, and discovered four hundred glassine packets containing heroin. Unfortunately, my partner Brit, the lieutenant, and narcotic squad detectives were outside and missed out on the three man wrestling tag team match versus the one man drug dealing suspect.

The suspect was advised, arrested for the above heroin and additional heroin found over his apartment door ledge. The Division of Youth and Family Services (D.Y.F.S.) was notified. They took the suspect's two children and left them in the custody of a relative. The suspect had been dealing large quantities of heroin out of his apartment, without being concerned with his children's presence or their safety. The suspect later indicated he picked up the VCR case because he was concerned that the police narcotics dog that was outside was coming in and would've sniffed out his stash. He figured his only chance was to pick it up, conceal it in his underwear, and somehow get us to allow him to use his bathroom, where he would've have dumped and flushed it. The drug dog made a bust on its mere presence and wasn't even awarded.

All you new and upcoming police officers, beware of that sudden, "Can I use the bathroom" move and watch those quick moving hands. Always allow your suspects to use the bathroom, relief room, john, toilet or whatever even if you have to disconnect the flush handle prior to them using it.

BRIT'S AND MY CAR CHASE

Brit and I were assigned together in uniform in a marked police vehicle and on the 1500 to 2300 hours shift. This particular evening we were on Bergen Street near Lyons Avenue with several other police units looking for a vehicle and suspects that were involved in a heinous crime. While on Bergen St. traveling southbound, a vehicle sped past us eastbound on Shephard Avenue and in doing so disregarded the stop sign. Brit immediately made a left turn and got behind the stop sign blowing vehicle. The vehicle made a sharp right turn onto Hunterdon Street and accelerated. I notified the dispatcher of our attempt to stop the vehicle that stole the stop sign (ran it) and that the driver was attempting to break and set a new speed and distance record. For some reason, maybe out of fear from hearing the power of our police vehicle's engine, on Lehigh Avenue, the suspect slowed down and threw a large caliber gun onto the street from the driver's door. He then turned the corner, stopped the vehicle, got out and ran into a vacant house. He was knocking down doors and shattering glass, as he attempted to create space between us and himself.

I exited our police vehicle at the point of where his loaded weapon was thrown and safe guarded the valuable evidence as Brit went after and chased the suspect on foot. Back up officers who were already in the area, quickly responded and the suspect was found and removed from the abandoned house. He was arrested for the unlawful possession of the firearm and unlawful drugs he still had in his pant's pocket he apparently forgot to get rid of while creating space. The only reason I can offer or think of as to why he threw the gun out of the car, continued on in the vehicle and then stopped the vehicle is that he had done it in the past and got away with it, and then returned and picked up the weapon. This was a situation where officers were already involved in a known risky situation and another risky situation crosses right in front of your eyes. If you're not wearing blinders, you'll see what you need to see. Also be willing to work, serve the public, be alert and, of course, follow your departmental guide lines. Sometimes those lines appear to curve when you're trying to be a top cop.

Another similar situation occurred when I was on patrol as a one man officer, and I attempted to pull over a vehicle for a traffic violation on Avon Avenue. The mechanically troubled vehicle refused to stop, sped off south on South Tenth Street with me in close pursuit. While the driver was trying to accelerate, the passenger threw out a loaded handgun. I had a choice to continue after them or stop and retrieve the weapon, and hope that back up officers would stop the fleeing vehicle. I did the right thing and got the weapon. The suspect vehicle got away. Most important was that somebody was probably allowed to keep their pay and/or live another day due to another unlawful handgun being taken off the streets, that day.

In case you've lost a little bit of interest in this book, this song hopefully will get you BACK on TRACK

BACK TRACK

Back track baby, Back track,
You may spin your wheels,
As if you're leaving me.
But I know, you ought to back track,
Back track baby, back track.
You may run in different circles of friends,
But I strongly suggest, before you get weak, running in circles
And passing out, what belongs to me.
You may want to strongly, reconsider
And back track baby, back track.
You may have a non stop, one directional, hot as motor,
Somehow you'll slow down, find reverse,
Cool off and be a cool as, you can be.
And back track baby, back track, back track it own back
to me.
Over that same still burning bridge, you fired up as you
crossed me.
I strongly suggest, before that bridge gets weak, with flames
burning in circles,
You fire that hot as motor up and
Back track baby, back track, back track.

Question: What do you call the folks in the below scenario?

Skip it if you're still interested in this book and would like to reread it.

MEN, WHEN YOUR "G/GIRL" IS ON THE BEACH, LYING IN THE SUN

AND SOME JOKER TRIES TO TOUCH HER BUN
AND YOU DON'T CONSIDER IT TO BE FUN.
BUT PLEASE, DON'T GO AND GET YOUR GUN,
IT'LL CAUSE YOU TO ALWAYS BE ON THE RUN.
ESPECIALLY IF THE JOKER LOOKS LIKE A HUN
AND HE WEIGHS TOO MUCH LIKE A TUN.
IF HE HITS YOU, YOU'RE TOO MUCH DUN
AND THERE'S NO WAY YOU COULD'VE WUN!

ANSWERS: If you didn't find them, don't worry about it. Standby for *Lock & Key Part II*

So Long For Now, It's Not The End.
AND PLEASE ALWAYS REMEMBER GOD'S FOREVER PRESENCE.